most loved recipe collection most loved recipe collection most loved recipe collection m
ved recipe collection most loved recipe collection most loved recipe collection most lo
tion most loved recipe collection most loved recipe collec... ...loved recipe collec
most loved recipe collection most loved recipe collection ...llection
on most loved recipe collection most loved recipe collec... ...e collecti
most loved recipe collection most loved recipe collection ...ection m
collection most loved recipe collection most loved recipe collection most loved recipe
tion most loved recipe collection most loved recipe collection most loved recipe collec
most loved recipe collection most loved recipe collection most loved recipe collection m
ved recipe collection most loved recipe collection most loved recipe collection most lo
tion most loved recipe collection most loved recipe collection most loved recipe collec
most loved recipe collection most loved recipe collection most loved recipe collection
on most loved recipe collection most loved recipe collection most loved recipe collecti
most loved recipe collection most loved recipe collection most loved recipe collection m
collection most loved recipe collection most loved recipe collection most loved recipe
tion most loved recipe collection most loved recipe collection most loved recipe collec
most loved recipe collection most loved recipe collection most loved recipe collection m
ved recipe collection most loved recipe collection most loved recipe collection most lo
tion most loved recipe collection most loved recipe collection most loved recipe collec
most loved recipe collection most loved recipe collection most loved recipe collection
on most loved recipe collection most loved recipe collection most loved recipe collecti
most loved recipe collection most loved recipe collection most loved recipe collection m
collection most loved recipe collection most loved recipe collection most loved recipe
tion most loved recipe collection most loved recipe collection most loved recipe collec
most loved recipe collection most loved recipe collection most loved recipe collection m
ved recipe collection most loved recipe collection most loved recipe collection most lo
tion most loved recipe collection most loved recipe collection most loved recipe collec
most loved recipe collection most loved recipe collection most loved recipe collection
on most loved recipe collection most loved recipe collection most loved recipe collecti
most loved recipe collection most loved recipe collection most loved recipe collection w
collection most loved recipe collection most loved recipe collection most loved recipe

most loved

main courses

Pictured on Front Cover:
Stuffed Roast With
  Red Wine Sauce, page 15

Pictured on Back Cover:
Sesame Chicken, page 106

Most Loved Main Courses

Copyright © Company's Coming Publishing Limited

First Printing April 2004

National Library of Canada Cataloguing in Publication
Paré, Jean
    Most loved main courses / Jean Paré.

(Most loved recipe collection)
Includes index.
ISBN 1-896891-78-0

    1. Entrées (Cookery) I. Title. II. Series.

TX740.P3482 2004   641.8'2   C2003-905240-0

Published by
COMPANY'S COMING PUBLISHING LIMITED
2311 – 96 Street
Edmonton, Alberta, Canada T6N 1G3
Tel: (780) 450-6223 Fax: (780) 450-1857
www.companyscoming.com

Company's Coming is a registered trademark owned by Company's Coming Publishing Limited

Colour separations by
Quality Colour, a division of Moore Corporation Limited, Edmonton, Alberta, Canada.

Printed in China

We gratefully acknowledge the following suppliers for their generous support of our Test Kitchen and Photo Studio:

Broil King Barbecues
Corelle®
Lagostina®
Tupperware®

Our special thanks to the following businesses for providing extensive props for photography:

Artifacts
Call The Kettle Black
Canhome Global
Casa Bugatti
Cherison Enterprises Inc.
Chintz & Company
Danesco Inc.
Dansk Gifts
IKEA
Island Pottery Inc.
Klass Works
La Cache
Le Gnome
Linens 'N Things
Mikasa Home Store
Pfaltzgraff Canada
Pier 1 Imports
Stokes
The Bay
Wiltshire®
Winners Stores

Pictured from left: Lemon Grass Pork, page 76; Beef Oscar, page 16; Aniseed Chicken, page 108; Orange And Dill Salmon, page 54

table of contents

the Company's Coming story

"never share a recipe you wouldn't use yourself"

Jean Paré grew up understanding that the combination of family, friends and home cooking is the essence of a good life. From her mother she learned to appreciate good cooking, while her father praised even her earliest attempts. When she left home she took with her many acquired family recipes, a love of cooking and an intriguing desire to read recipe books like novels!

In 1963, when her four children had all reached school age, Jean volunteered to cater the 50th anniversary of the Vermilion School of Agriculture, now Lakeland College. Working out of her home, Jean prepared a dinner for over 1000 people which launched a flourishing catering operation that continued for over eighteen years. During that time she was provided with countless opportunities to test new ideas with immediate feedback—resulting in empty plates and contented customers! Whether preparing cocktail sandwiches for a house party or serving a hot meal for 1500 people, Jean Paré earned a reputation for good food, courteous service and reasonable prices.

"Why don't you write a cookbook?" Time and again, as requests for her recipes mounted, Jean was asked that question. Jean's response was to team up with her son, Grant Lovig, in the fall of 1980 to form Company's Coming Publishing Limited. April 14, 1981 marked the debut of "150 DELICIOUS SQUARES," the first Company's Coming cookbook in what soon would become Canada's most popular cookbook series.

Jean Paré's operation has grown steadily from the early days of working out of a spare bedroom in her home. Full-time staff includes marketing personnel located in major cities across Canada. Home Office is based in Edmonton, Alberta in a modern building constructed specially for the company.

Today the company distributes throughout Canada and the United States in addition to numerous overseas markets, all under the guidance of Jean's daughter, Gail Lovig. Best-sellers many times over in English, Company's Coming cookbooks have also been published in French and Spanish. Familiar and trusted in home kitchens around the world, Company's Coming cookbooks are offered in a variety of formats, including the original softcover series.

Jean Paré's approach to cooking has always called for quick and easy recipes using everyday ingredients. Even when travelling, she is constantly on the lookout for new ideas to share with her readers. At home, she can usually be found researching and writing recipes, or working in the company's test kitchen. Jean continues to gain new supporters by adhering to what she calls "the golden rule of cooking:" never share a recipe you wouldn't use yourself. It's an approach that works—*millions of times over!*

foreword

Now you can find your favourite Company's Coming main course dishes in one convenient collection! *Most Loved Main Courses* offers over eighty mealtime ideas, perfect for those with a busy, on-the-go lifestyle. With this book on your shelf, you can relax, as you'll always have something delicious to prepare for friends and family. Because these time-tested recipes call for common, everyday ingredients, you can create a complete meal in no time! We've also included helpful time saver tips so you can spend your valuable time doing the things that are really important—cherishing family moments and visiting with friends.

Because the main course is the focal point of the meal, you want it to be special. Whether it's a casual, relaxed dinner or a more formal gathering, you can prepare these dishes with confidence. With dozens of tips and so many tried-and-true recipes, you're sure to achieve great results every time.

Most Loved Main Courses is organized into sections based on the main meat component in the dish. Whether you're in the mood for beef, fish, seafood, pork, lamb or poultry, you'll find many enticing options in this book. Complement your main course dish by serving it with fresh bread and a nice wine, or for a more casual meal, add a garden salad and some fresh rolls. Where appropriate, we've listed serving suggestions to inspire your imagination.

When lots of laughter, great food and a comfortable atmosphere are combined, your meal will always be a success. Keep these traditions alive and take pleasure in sharing your mealtime triumphs with family and friends!

Jean Paré

nutrition information

Each recipe has been analyzed using the most up-to-date version of the Canadian Nutrient File from Health Canada, which is based on the United States Department of Agriculture (USDA) Nutrient Data Base. If more than one ingredient is listed (such as "hard margarine or butter"), then the first ingredient is used in the analysis. Where an ingredient reads "sprinkle," "optional," or "for garnish," it is not included as part of the nutrition information.

Margaret Ng, B.Sc. (Hon.), M.A.
Registered Dietitian

The sauce is very tasty and the perfect complement to the tender roast.

Peppercorn Roast

Beef inside round (or rump or sirloin tip) roast	3 1/2 lbs.	1.6 kg
Dijon mustard	2 tbsp.	30 mL
Lemon juice	1 tbsp.	15 mL
Crushed whole peppercorns (or coarse ground pepper)	2 tsp.	10 mL
Ground cloves	1/2 tsp.	2 mL
Dried whole oregano	1/2 tsp.	2 mL
HORSERADISH SAUCE		
Sour cream	1 cup	250 mL
Grated fresh horseradish, drained	1 tbsp.	15 mL
Dijon mustard	1 tbsp.	15 mL
Lemon juice	1 tsp.	5 mL
Salt, sprinkle		
Pepper, sprinkle		

Place roast in large bowl.

Combine next 5 ingredients in small cup. Rub over entire surface of roast. Cover. Chill overnight. Preheat gas barbecue to medium. Turn off centre or left burner. Place roast on greased grill over drip pan on unlit side. Close lid. Cook for about 2 1/2 hours until meat thermometer reads 155°F (68°C) for medium or until desired doneness. Let stand, tented with foil, for 15 minutes before cutting.

Horseradish Sauce: Combine all 6 ingredients in small bowl. Mix well. Makes 1 cup (250 mL) sauce. Serve with roast. Makes fourteen 3 oz. (85 g) servings.

1 serving: 159 Calories; 7.3 g Total Fat (2.6 g Mono, 0.5 g Poly, 3.2 g Sat); 52 mg Cholesterol; 1 g Carbohydrate; trace Fibre; 21 g Protein; 90 mg Sodium

Pictured on page 7.

Enjoy the delicious blend of spices in this tender roast.

note

Use any leftover tenderloin the next day in sandwiches.

Herbed Beef Tenderloin

Beef tenderloin roast	3 lbs.	1.4 kg
Olive (or cooking) oil	2 tsp.	10 mL
Parsley flakes	2 tsp.	10 mL
Dried thyme	1 1/2 tsp.	7 mL
Dried tarragon	1 tsp.	5 mL
Onion powder	1 tsp.	5 mL
Garlic powder	1/2 tsp.	2 mL
Salt	1/4 tsp.	1 mL
Coarse ground pepper	1 tsp.	5 mL

If necessary, tuck thin end of roast underneath to make shape as uniform as possible. Tie lengthwise, then crosswise, with butcher's string to hold. Rub olive oil over entire surface of roast.

Combine remaining 7 ingredients in small cup. Rub over entire surface of roast. Place roast on rack in broiler pan. Bake, uncovered, in 425°F (220°C) oven for about 45 minutes until meat thermometer reads 155°F (68°C) for medium or until desired doneness. Let stand, tented with foil, for 15 minutes before cutting. Makes twelve 3 oz. (85 g) servings.

1 serving: 218 Calories; 11.2 g Total Fat (4.8 g Mono, 0.6 g Poly, 3.9 g Sat); 65 mg Cholesterol; 1 g Carbohydrate; trace Fibre; 27 g Protein; 145 mg Sodium

Pictured on page 9.

The beer in the marinade adds a wonderful flavour.

make ahead

Marinate overnight. Allow about 1 1/2 hours to barbecue and make sauce.

note

You will need to special order this thickness of steak from your butcher.

A Round Of Draft

Beef inside round steak (2 inches, 5 cm, thick), see Note	3 lbs.	1.4 kg
BEER MARINADE		
Can of regular beer	12 1/2 oz.	355 mL
Cooking oil	1/4 cup	60 mL
Apple cider vinegar	2 tbsp.	30 mL
Brown sugar, packed	2 tbsp.	30 mL
Medium onion, thinly sliced	1	1
Garlic cloves, minced (or 1/2 tsp., 2 mL, powder)	2	2
Bay leaf	1	1
Ground thyme	1/2 tsp.	2 mL
Salt	1/2 tsp.	2 mL
Coarse ground pepper	1/4 tsp.	1 mL

Brown sugar, pinch

Pierce steak in several places with thin metal skewer or fork. Place in shallow dish.

Beer Marinade: Combine first 10 ingredients in small bowl. Pour over steak. Turn to coat. Cover. Marinate in refrigerator for 8 hours or overnight, turning several times. Drain, reserving marinade. Boil marinade in small saucepan for 5 minutes.

Preheat gas barbecue to high. Place steak on greased grill. Close lid. Cook for 4 minutes per side. Turn off centre or left burner. Move steak to unlit side. Close lid. Cook over medium heat for about 1 hour until meat thermometer reads 155°F (68°C) for medium or until desired doneness, brushing twice with reserved marinade. Discard bay leaf from remaining marinade. Remove onion from marinade to non-stick frying pan. Add second amount of brown sugar. Stir. Cook on medium, stirring occasionally, until onion is softened. Pour in remaining marinade. Boil until reduced by 1/3. Cut steak across grain into 1/2 inch (12 mm) strips. Top with onion mixture. Makes twelve 3 oz. (85 g) servings.

1 serving: 186 Calories; 7.3 g Total Fat (3.8 g Mono, 1.5 g Poly, 1.3 g Sat); 43 mg Cholesterol; 5 g Carbohydrate; trace Fibre; 22 g Protein; 163 mg Sodium

Pictured on page 11.

Tender, moist roast slowly cooked in a rich, brown gravy.

Slow Cooker Beef Roast

Boneless beef sirloin tip roast	3 – 4 lbs.	1.4 – 1.8 kg
Envelope of dry onion soup mix	1 1/2 oz.	42 g
Envelope of brown gravy mix	1 1/8 oz.	32 g
Lemon lime soft drink	2 cups	500 mL
BEEFY ONION GRAVY		
Water		
Water	2/3 cup	150 mL
All-purpose flour	1/2 cup	125 mL

Place roast in 3 1/2 quart (3.5 L) slow cooker.

Combine soup mix, gravy mix and soft drink in small bowl. Pour over roast. Cover. Cook on Low for 8 to 10 hours or on High for 4 to 5 hours until tender. Remove roast to serving platter.

Beefy Onion Gravy: Pour drippings into 4 cup (1 L) liquid measure. Let stand for about 10 minutes until fat separates and rises to surface. Carefully spoon off fat and discard. Add water to drippings to make 4 cups (1 L). Pour into large saucepan or roasting pan. Bring to a boil on medium.

Stir second amount of water into flour in small bowl until smooth. Stir into drippings. Heat and stir for 5 to 7 minutes, until boiling and thickened. Makes about 4 cups (1 L) gravy. Serve with roast. Makes twelve 3 oz. (85 g) servings.

1 serving: 215 Calories; 6.3 g Total Fat (2.7 g Mono, 0.4 g Poly, 2.3 g Sat); 55 mg Cholesterol; 12 g Carbohydrate; trace Fibre; 26 g Protein; 465 mg Sodium

Pictured on page 13.

Top: Spicy Stuffed Beef, page 14
Bottom: Slow Cooker Beef Roast, above

The mild stuffing inside is complemented by the spicy rub outside.

Spicy Stuffed Beef

RAISIN 'N' BREAD STUFFING

Fresh coarse bread crumbs	2 cups	500 mL
Chopped raisins	1/2 cup	125 mL
Chopped water chestnuts (1/2 of 8 oz., 227 mL, can)	1/2 cup	125 mL
Chopped green onion	1/4 cup	60 mL
Hard margarine (or butter), melted	3 tbsp.	50 mL
Chopped fresh thyme leaves (or 3/4 tsp., 4 mL, dried)	1 tbsp.	15 mL
Boneless beef rib-eye roast	2 – 2 1/2 lbs.	900 g – 1.1 kg

ONION HERB RUB

Brown sugar, packed	2 tbsp.	30 mL
Onion powder	1 tbsp.	15 mL
Paprika	1 tbsp.	15 mL
Garlic powder	2 tsp.	10 mL
Salt	1/2 tsp.	2 mL
Pepper	1/2 tsp.	2 mL

Raisin 'N' Bread Stuffing: Combine first 6 ingredients in medium bowl. Makes 3 cups (750 mL) stuffing.

Cut deep pocket into long side of roast almost through to other side. Spoon stuffing into pocket. Tie roast with butcher's string at 1 inch (2.5 cm) intervals.

Onion Herb Rub: Combine all 6 ingredients in small cup. Makes about 1/3 cup (75 mL) rub. Rub over entire surface of roast. Preheat gas barbecue to high. Turn off centre or left burner. Place roast on greased grill over drip pan on unlit side. Close lid. Cook for 35 minutes. Turn roast. Cook for 40 to 45 minutes until meat thermometer reads 155°F (68°C) for medium or until desired doneness. Let stand, tented with foil, for 15 minutes before cutting into 1/2 inch (12 mm) thick slices. Makes eight to ten 3 oz. (85 g) servings.

1 serving: 394 Calories; 15.7 g Total Fat (7.6 g Mono, 1.3 g Poly, 5.2 g Sat); 51 mg Cholesterol; 37 g Carbohydrate; 2 g Fibre; 26 g Protein; 495 mg Sodium

Pictured on page 13.

Stuffed Roast With Red Wine Sauce

Cooking oil	2 tsp.	10 mL
Small onion, finely chopped	1	1
Bacon slices, finely chopped	3	3
Coarse dry bread crumbs	2 cups	500 mL
Chopped fresh parsley (or 2 1/4 tsp., 11 mL, flakes)	3 tbsp.	50 mL
Creamed horseradish	2 tbsp.	30 mL
Coarse ground pepper	1 tsp.	5 mL
Beef top sirloin roast	4 1/2 lbs.	2 kg
Water	1/2 cup	125 mL
RED WINE SAUCE		
All-purpose flour	1/4 cup	60 mL
Prepared beef broth	2 cups	500 mL
Dry red (or alcohol-free) wine	1 cup	250 mL
Creamed horseradish	2 tbsp.	30 mL
Salt, sprinkle		
Freshly ground pepper, sprinkle		

Heat cooking oil in medium frying pan on medium-high. Add onion. Cook for 5 to 10 minutes, stirring often, until softened.

Add bacon. Cook for about 5 minutes until bacon is crisp. Do not drain.

Combine next 4 ingredients in medium bowl. Add bacon mixture. Mix well.

Cut deep pocket into long side of roast almost through to other side. Spoon stuffing into pocket. Tie with butcher's string at 1 1/4 inch (3 cm) intervals. Place roast on greased rack in roasting pan. Pour water into bottom of pan. Roast, uncovered, in 350°F (175°C) oven for about 1 3/4 hours until meat thermometer reads 155°F (68°C) for medium or until desired doneness. Let stand, tented with foil, for 15 minutes before cutting into 1/2 inch (12 mm) slices.

Red Wine Sauce: Drain all but 2 tbsp. (30 mL) drippings from roasting pan. Stir in flour until smooth. Heat and stir on medium for about 1 minute until grainy.

Add remaining 5 ingredients. Heat and stir for 10 to 12 minutes, until boiling and thickened. Strain. Makes about 1 1/4 cups (300 mL) sauce. Serve drizzled over beef slices. Makes seventeen 3 oz. (85 g) servings.

1 serving: 268 Calories; 9.4 g Total Fat (4.6 g Mono, 1 g Poly, 3.5 g Sat); 60 mg Cholesterol; 12 g Carbohydrate; 1 g Fibre; 30 g Protein; 322 mg Sodium

Pictured on front cover.

Never underestimate the appeal of perfectly roasted beef at any special occasion. It has everything it takes to please a crowd and make the cook a hero. In this presentation, an unusually good stuffing, flavoured with horseradish and bacon, pairs beautifully with an au jus-like wine sauce.

serving suggestion

Serve with roasted baby potatoes, carrots and pearl onions.

Decadent and rich with lots of sauce.

serving suggestion

Serve with roasted red baby potatoes seasoned with dill.

veal oscar

Omit beef. Use same amount of veal.

Beef Oscar

Fresh asparagus spears, trimmed of tough ends	16	16
Water		
Can of crabmeat, drained and cartilage removed	4 1/4 oz.	120 g
All-purpose flour	1/4 cup	60 mL
Salt	1/2 tsp.	2 mL
Pepper	1/8 tsp.	0.5 mL
Beef tenderloin steaks (about 4 oz., 113 g, each)	4	4
Hard margarine (or butter)	2 tsp.	10 mL
Cooking oil	2 tsp.	10 mL
JIFFY HOLLANDAISE SAUCE		
Egg yolks (large)	3	3
Lemon juice	2 tbsp.	30 mL
Salt	1/4 tsp.	1 mL
Hot pepper sauce	1/16 tsp.	0.5 mL
Butter (not hard margarine)	3/4 cup	175 mL

Freshly ground pepper, for garnish
Chopped fresh parsley, for garnish

Cook asparagus in water in large saucepan until tender. Drain. Keep hot.

Heat crab in small saucepan or in microwave. Keep hot.

Combine flour, salt and pepper in shallow dish or on waxed paper.

Flatten steaks with meat mallet. Coat with flour mixture. Melt margarine in cooking oil in frying pan on medium. Add steaks to frying pan. Cook for 3 to 4 minutes per side until desired doneness. Transfer to 4 individual serving plates. Place 4 asparagus spears on each steak. Divide crab over asparagus. Keep warm.

Jiffy Hollandaise Sauce: Process egg yolks, lemon juice, salt and pepper sauce in blender for 5 to 6 seconds until smooth.

(continued on next page)

Heat butter in small saucepan until bubbling. With motor running, very slowly pour butter through hole in blender lid. Process until fluffy and thick. Makes 1 cup (250 mL) sauce. Divide and spoon sauce over each serving.

Garnish with pepper and parsley. Serves 4.

1 serving: 651 Calories; 53.2 g Total Fat (17.8 g Mono, 3.3 g Poly, 27.6 g Sat); 341 mg Cholesterol; 10 g Carbohydrate; 1 g Fibre; 34 g Protein; 1000 mg Sodium

Pictured below.

Fussy to make, but fast to bake. Mild-tasting tender beef in a golden packet. Simply wonderful!

Beef In Pastry

Olive (or cooking) oil	2 tsp.	10 mL
Fresh mushrooms, finely chopped	1/2 lb.	225 g
Dry red (or alcohol-free) wine	3 tbsp.	50 mL
Finely chopped green onion	1/4 cup	60 mL
Dried thyme	1/4 tsp.	1 mL
Salt	1/4 tsp.	1 mL
Pepper	1/8 tsp.	0.5 mL
Beef tenderloin steaks (about 4 oz., 113 g, each), 1 inch (2.5 cm) thick	4	4
Salt, sprinkle		
Pepper, sprinkle		
Frozen phyllo pastry sheets, thawed according to package directions	6	6

Heat olive oil in frying pan on medium. Add mushrooms. Heat and stir until tender. Add wine. Stir. Cook for about 2 minutes until liquid is evaporated.

Add green onion, thyme and first amounts of salt and pepper. Stir. Remove from frying pan. Cool thoroughly.

Sear steaks in same frying pan on medium-high for 1 1/2 minutes per side. Steaks will only be partially cooked. Do not overcook. Sprinkle with second amounts of salt and pepper.

Spray 1 side of each phyllo sheet thoroughly with cooking spray. Stack into 1 pile on flat surface. Cut lengthwise in half and then crosswise in half to make 4 stacks. Divide and spoon mushroom mixture onto centre of each stack. Spread slightly in centre to size of each steak. Place steaks on mushroom mixture. Bring all 4 corners of each phyllo packet together. Pinch and twist tightly to close. Lightly spray each packet with cooking spray. Place on lightly greased baking sheet. Bake in 425°F (220°C) oven for 9 to 10 minutes until golden. Let stand for 5 minutes before serving. Serves 4.

1 serving: 318 Calories; 17.1 g Total Fat (8.1 g Mono, 2.2 g Poly, 4.9 g Sat); 55 mg Cholesterol; 13 g Carbohydrate; 1 g Fibre; 25 g Protein; 362 mg Sodium

Pictured on page 19.

The taste of these juicy, grilled steaks is complemented by a delicious sesame seed and curry coating. Top with the uniquely flavoured salsa for a sensational dinner treat.

Steak With Spice Coating

Sesame seeds	2 tbsp.	30 mL
Curry powder	1 tbsp.	15 mL
Coarse ground pepper	2 tsp.	10 mL
Beef tenderloin steaks (about 4 oz., 113 g, each), 1 inch (2.5 cm) thick	4	4
PAPAYA COCONUT SALSA		
Chopped ripe papaya	1 cup	250 mL
Flake coconut, toasted (see Note)	1/4 cup	60 mL
Sweet (or regular) chili sauce	2 tbsp.	30 mL
Chopped fresh mint leaves (or 3/4 – 1 1/2 tsp., 4 – 7 mL, dried)	1 – 2 tbsp.	15 – 30 mL
White wine vinegar	1 tbsp.	15 mL

Combine sesame seeds, curry powder and pepper in shallow dish.

Preheat lightly greased electric grill for 5 minutes. Roll edge of each steak in sesame seed mixture until coated. Place steaks on grill. Cook for 5 to 7 minutes per side until desired doneness.

Papaya Coconut Salsa: Combine all 5 ingredients in small bowl. Makes 1 1/4 cups (300 mL) salsa. Serve with steaks. Serves 4.

1 serving: 267 Calories; 13.8 g Total Fat (4.1 g Mono, 1.3 g Poly, 6.3 g Sat); 70 mg Cholesterol; 10 g Carbohydrate; 3 g Fibre; 25 g Protein; 302 mg Sodium

Pictured on page 21.

Grilled steak topped with a slightly sweet, garlic-flavoured butter and shrimp.

Buttered Steak And Shrimp

HONEY MUSTARD BUTTER

Cooking oil	2 tsp.	10 mL
Finely chopped red onion	2 tbsp.	30 mL
Garlic clove, minced (or 1/4 tsp., 1 mL, powder)	1	1
Hard margarine (or butter), softened	1/3 cup	75 mL
Honey mustard	2 tbsp.	30 mL
Chopped fresh parsley (or 3/4 – 1 1/2 tsp., 4 – 7 mL, flakes)	1 – 2 tbsp.	15 – 30 mL
Pepper	1/4 tsp.	1 mL
Beef rib-eye medallions (filet mignon), about 4 oz. (113 g) each	4	4
Cooking oil	1 tbsp.	15 mL
Salt	1/4 tsp.	1 mL
Pepper	1/4 tsp.	1 mL
Raw large shrimp (tails intact), peeled and deveined	12	12

Honey Mustard Butter: Heat first amount of cooking oil in small saucepan on medium-low. Add onion and garlic. Cook for about 5 minutes, stirring often, until onion is softened. Put into small bowl. Cool.

Add next 4 ingredients. Stir until well combined. Shape into 4 inch (10 cm) log on waxed paper. Wrap. Chill for 1 to 2 hours until firm. Cut into 1/2 inch (12 mm) rounds.

Brush both sides of each medallion with second amount of cooking oil. Sprinkle with salt and second amount of pepper. Preheat gas barbecue to medium-high. Place steaks on greased grill. Cook for about 7 minutes per side for medium or until desired doneness.

Cook shrimp on greased grill for about 2 minutes per side until pink and curled. Do not overcook. Place 2 rounds of butter and 3 shrimp on top of each hot steak. Serves 4.

1 serving: 504 Calories; 36.8 g Total Fat (14.3 g Mono, 3.1 g Poly, 16.3 g Sat); 152 mg Cholesterol; 6 g Carbohydrate; trace Fibre; 37 g Protein; 464 mg Sodium

Pictured on page 23.

Visually appealing and tasty with a nice mustard flavour.

Broiled Herbed Rouladen

Dijon mustard	2 tbsp.	30 mL
Beef rouladen steaks (about 4 oz., 113 g, each) or top round slices (1/4 inch, 6 mm, thick)	2	2
Finely chopped fresh parsley (or 1 1/2 tsp., 7 mL, flakes)	2 tbsp.	30 mL

Spread mustard on 1 side of each steak. Sprinkle with parsley. Roll up, jelly roll-style. Secure with wooden picks. Place rolls on ungreased rack in broiler pan. Broil, seam-side down, on top rack in oven for 4 minutes. Turn. Broil for 3 minutes. Do not overcook. Slice each roll into 1/4 inch (6 mm) slices. Serves 2.

1 serving: 142 Calories; 3.9 g Total Fat (1.4 g Mono, 0.7 g Poly, 1.2 g Sat); 46 mg Cholesterol; 1 g Carbohydrate; trace Fibre; 25 g Protein; 261 mg Sodium

Pictured on page 26/27.

Delicate orange flavour with a hint of soy sauce. Ready in less than 30 minutes.

Zesty Broiled Steak

Soy sauce	1 tbsp.	15 mL
Garlic clove, minced (or 1/4 tsp., 1 mL, powder)	1	1
Finely grated orange zest	1 tsp.	5 mL
Dried rosemary, crushed	1/2 tsp.	2 mL
Beef sirloin (or rib-eye or strip loin) steak (3/4 inch, 2 cm, thick)	1/2 lb.	225 g
Sesame seeds, toasted (see Note)		

Combine first 4 ingredients in small cup.

Brush both sides of steak with soy sauce mixture. Let stand for 10 minutes to absorb flavours. Place on ungreased rack in broiler pan. Broil on top rack in oven for 4 to 6 minutes per side until desired doneness.

Sprinkle with sesame seeds. Serves 2.

1 serving: 142 Calories; 4.1 g Total Fat (2 g Mono, 0.5 g Poly, 1.7 g Sat); 53 mg Cholesterol; 2 g Carbohydrate; trace Fibre; 23 g Protein; 571 mg Sodium

Pictured on page 26.

Acapulco Beef Filet

Hard margarine (or butter)	1 tbsp.	15 mL
Large onion, cut lengthwise into slivers	1	1
Red medium pepper, cut into 1 1/2 inch (3.8 cm) pieces	1	1
Yellow medium pepper, cut into 1 1/2 inch (3.8 cm) pieces	1	1
Chili sauce	3 tbsp.	50 mL
Condensed beef broth	1/2 cup	125 mL
Salt	1/2 tsp.	2 mL
Coarse ground pepper	1 tsp.	5 mL
Beef tenderloin steaks (about 4 oz., 113 g, each)	4	4
Coarse ground pepper	2 tsp.	10 mL
Cooking oil	1 tbsp.	15 mL
Tequila	2 tbsp.	30 mL
Lime juice	1 tbsp.	15 mL
Salt	1/4 tsp.	1 mL

Tender beef coated in a wonderful smooth, red sauce.

time saver

Have two frying pans going at once to save time.

Melt margarine in frying pan on medium. Add onion. Cook for about 10 minutes, stirring often, until golden.

Add red and yellow peppers. Heat and stir for 2 to 3 minutes until tender-crisp.

Add next 4 ingredients. Cover. Simmer for 7 minutes. Drain. Transfer to serving platter. Keep warm.

Blot steaks with paper towels. Divide and rub second amount of pepper into both sides of each steak with heel of hand.

Heat cooking oil in cast-iron frying pan until very hot. Add steaks. Sear for 3 to 4 minutes per side until desired doneness. Place steaks on top of warm pepper mixture.

Combine tequila and lime juice in same frying pan. Simmer, uncovered, for 2 minutes. Add second amount of salt. Stir. Pour sauce over steaks. Serves 4.

1 serving: 271 Calories; 13.7 g Total Fat (6.6 g Mono, 1.7 g Poly, 3.5 g Sat); 55 mg Cholesterol; 7 g Carbohydrate; 1 g Fibre; 25 g Protein; 768 mg Sodium

Pictured on page 27.

Pictured on Next Page:
Top Left: Zesty Broiled Steak, page 24
Top Right: Acapulco Beef Filet, this page
Bottom: Broiled Herbed Rouladen, page 24

Filet Mignon wrapped in bacon. A pricey treat, but worth it.

note

When cooking steak, turn over without piercing so that juices remain in steak.

serving suggestion

Serve with steamed herbed potatoes and steamed carrots.

presentation idea

For a fancy look, cut a star shape into the mushroom cap with a paring knife before cooking.

Tournados

Bacon slices	6	6
Beef tenderloin steaks (about 4 oz., 113 g, each), 1 1/4 – 1 1/2 inches (3 – 4 cm) thick	6	6
Hard margarine (butter browns too fast)	2 tbsp.	30 mL
Pepper, sprinkle		
Hard margarine (or butter), optional	2 tbsp.	30 mL
Large mushroom caps	6	6
Bread slices	6	6

Wrap 1 slice of bacon around circumference of each steak. Secure with wooden pick.

Melt margarine in frying pan on medium. Add steaks. Cook for about 5 minutes per side until desired doneness.

Sprinkle with pepper. Remove bacon-wrapped steaks to plate. Cover to keep hot.

Melt second amount of margarine in same frying pan on medium. Add mushrooms. Cook, stirring often, until liquid is evaporated. Remove to bowl.

Cut bread into circles slightly larger than steaks. Add to same frying pan. Cook both sides until browned. Remove to 6 individual plates. Place steaks on top of bread rounds. Top each steak with 1 mushroom cap. Serves 6.

1 serving: 305 Calories; 15.3 g Total Fat (7.2 g Mono, 1.2 g Poly, 4.9 g Sat); 64 mg Cholesterol; 12 g Carbohydrate; trace Fibre; 28 g Protein; 322 mg Sodium

Pictured on page 29.

The hotter the salsa, the hotter the surprise.

Salsa-Stuffed Steak

Beef sirloin (or strip loin or rib-eye) steak (3/4 – 1 inch, 2 – 2.5 cm, thick)	1 1/2 lbs.	680 g

(continued on next page)

Salsa	1/2 cup	125 mL
Garlic cloves, minced (or 1/2 tsp., 2 mL, powder)	2	2
Small onion, finely chopped	1	1
Ground cumin (or dried whole oregano)	1 tsp.	5 mL
Pepper	1 tsp.	5 mL

Cut steak into 4 portions. Cut deep pocket into 1 side of each portion.

Combine salsa, garlic and onion in small bowl. Divide and stuff salsa mixture into each pocket. Close opening with skewer. Sprinkle with cumin and pepper. Preheat gas barbecue to medium-low. Place stuffed steak pieces on greased grill. Cook for 5 to 7 minutes per side until desired doneness. Serves 4.

1 serving: 224 Calories; 6.4 g Total Fat (2.7 g Mono, 0.3 g Poly, 2.4 g Sat); 80 mg Cholesterol; 6 g Carbohydrate; 1 g Fibre; 35 g Protein; 118 mg Sodium

Pictured below.

note

Prepare in just ten minutes.

serving suggestion

Steamed rice with diced peppers complement this dish very well.

Top Left: Tournados, page 28
Bottom Right: Salsa-Stuffed Steak, page 28

Enhance the flavour of commercial Italian dressing and you have a marinade that's quick to prepare.

Steak With Mushrooms And Onions

MARINADE

Italian dressing	1/2 cup	125 mL
Red wine vinegar	2 tbsp.	30 mL
Garlic clove, minced (or 1/4 tsp., 1 mL, powder)	1	1
Freshly ground pepper, sprinkle		
Whole portobello mushrooms (about 4 inches, 10 cm, diameter)	2	2
Large red (or Spanish) onion, cut into thick slices	1	1
Beef top sirloin steak	1 lb.	454 g
Seasoned salt	1/2 tsp.	2 mL
Freshly ground pepper, sprinkle		

Marinade: Combine first 4 ingredients in glass pie plate.

Remove stems from mushrooms and reserve for another purpose. Scrape and discard black "gills" from around underside of mushrooms with spoon. Place mushrooms in marinade. Turn to coat. Marinate in refrigerator for 30 minutes. Drain, reserving marinade. Boil marinade in small saucepan for 5 minutes.

Preheat lightly greased electric grill for 5 minutes. Place mushrooms and onion on grill. Cook for 7 to 8 minutes, turning and basting with marinade several times, until onion is tender-crisp. Remove to medium bowl.

Sear steak on grill for 1 minute per side. Sprinkle both sides with seasoned salt and pepper. Dab with marinade. Cook for 3 to 4 minutes per side until desired doneness. Discard any remaining marinade. Cut into thin slices across grain. Arrange on platter. Cut mushrooms into thin slices. Cut onion slices into quarters. Arrange over top of steak to serve. Serves 4.

1 serving: 325 Calories; 23.9 g Total Fat (12.5 g Mono, 6.8 g Poly, 3 g Sat); 64 mg Cholesterol; 9 g Carbohydrate; 2 g Fibre; 20 g Protein; 651 mg Sodium

Pictured on page 31.

Top Right: Steak With Mushrooms And Onions, above
Bottom Left: Beef Bourguignon, page 32

Serve this well-known dish complete with gravy.

note

To peel pearl onions, blanch quickly in boiling water, then peel.

serving suggestion

Serve over egg noodles.

Beef Bourguignon

Ingredient	Imperial	Metric
Hard margarine (or butter)	2 tbsp.	30 mL
Cooking oil	2 tbsp.	30 mL
Boneless beef chuck (or rump) steak, cut into 1 inch (2.5 cm) cubes	2 lbs.	900 g
Fresh small mushrooms	1/2 lb.	225 g
All-purpose flour	1/4 cup	60 mL
Hard margarine (or butter), optional	2 tbsp.	30 mL
Salt	1/2 tsp.	2 mL
Pepper	1/2 tsp.	2 mL
Burgundy (or alcohol-free red) wine	2 cups	500 mL
Garlic clove, minced (or 1/4 tsp., 1 mL, powder)	1	1
Bay leaf	1	1
Ketchup	1 tbsp.	15 mL
Parsley flakes	1 tsp.	5 mL
Thyme	1/2 tsp.	2 mL
Beef bouillon cubes (1/5 oz., 6 g, each)	3	3
Boiling water	1 cup	250 mL
Tiny white pearl onions, peeled (see Note)	1 1/2 cups	375 mL

Melt margarine in cooking oil in frying pan on medium-high. Add beef. Heat and stir until browned. Transfer to large saucepan.

Put mushrooms into same frying pan. Heat and stir for 3 to 4 minutes until liquid is evaporated. Add to beef.

Combine next 4 ingredients in same frying pan until smooth.

Add next 6 ingredients. Heat and stir until boiling and thickened.

Dissolve bouillon cubes in boiling water. Add to wine mixture. Stir. Pour over beef mixture. Cover. Simmer for 1 hour.

Add onions. Cover. Simmer for about 30 minutes until tender. Discard bay leaf. Serves 6.

1 serving: 405 Calories; 19.9 g Total Fat (8.8 g Mono, 2 g Poly, 7 g Sat); 90 mg Cholesterol; 11 g Carbohydrate; trace Fibre; 31 g Protein; 1077 mg Sodium

Pictured on page 31.

Swiss Stew

Cooking oil	2 tbsp.	30 mL
Beef inside round steak, cut into 1 1/2 inch (3.8 cm) cubes	2 lbs.	1 kg
Garlic powder, sprinkle		
Salt, sprinkle		
Pepper, sprinkle		
Can of stewed tomatoes	14 oz.	398 mL
Can of mushroom pieces (with liquid)	10 oz.	284 mL
Can of tomato paste	5 1/2 oz.	156 mL
Medium onion, cut into 1 1/2 inch (3.8 cm) pieces	1	1
Celery ribs, cut into 1 1/2 inch (3.8 cm) pieces	4 – 6	4 – 6

Heat cooking oil in large frying pan on medium. Add beef. Sprinkle with garlic powder, salt and pepper. Cook for 2 to 3 minutes, stirring often, until browned. Remove to ungreased 3 quart (3 L) casserole or small roaster.

Add tomatoes, mushrooms and tomato paste to same frying pan. Stir to combine, being sure to get brown bits from bottom of pan. Add onion and celery. Stir. Pour over beef. Stir. Cover. Bake in 350°F (175°C) oven for 2 to 2 1/2 hours until beef is very tender. Serves 8.

1 serving: 268 Calories; 9.3 g Total Fat (2.3 g Mono, 3.3 g Poly, 2.6 g Sat); 50 mg Cholesterol; 17 g Carbohydrate; 2 g Fibre; 29 g Protein; 1007 mg Sodium

Pictured on page 35.

A good take along dish anytime, anywhere.

serving suggestion

Complete the meal with hearty crusty buns.

The sweetness of the raisins and yam complements the nutty flavour of peanut butter sauce.

note

When a recipe calls for only a portion of a can of tomato paste, freeze the can for 30 minutes. Open both ends and push contents through with one end, slicing off only what you need. Freeze the rest of the contents in plastic wrap for future use.

serving suggestion

Serve with whole wheat crusty buns.

Beef And Yam Stew

Peanut (or cooking) oil	1 tbsp.	15 mL
Beef inside round (or blade or chuck) steak, cut into 1 inch (2.5 cm) cubes	2 lbs.	900 g
Peanut (or cooking) oil	1 tbsp.	15 mL
Large onion, chopped	1	1
Garlic powder	1 tsp.	5 mL
Ground coriander	2 – 3 tsp.	10 – 15 mL
Chili powder	1/2 – 1 tsp.	2 – 5 mL
Prepared beef broth	2 cups	500 mL
Tomato paste (see Note)	1/4 cup	60 mL
Cubed yam (or sweet potato), about 1 inch (2.5 cm) pieces	2 cups	500 mL
Raisins	2/3 cup	150 mL
Salt	1/2 tsp.	2 mL
Pepper	1/2 tsp.	2 mL
Smooth peanut butter	1/3 cup	75 mL
Fresh spinach, stems removed	1 1/2 cups	375 mL

Heat first amount of peanut oil in large pot or Dutch oven on medium-high. Add beef. Cook, in 2 to 3 batches, until browned on all sides. Remove from pot.

Heat second amount of peanut oil in same pot on medium. Add onion. Cook for 5 to 10 minutes, stirring often, until softened.

Add garlic powder, coriander and chili powder. Heat and stir for 1 to 2 minutes until fragrant.

Add beef, broth and tomato paste. Stir. Bring to a boil. Reduce heat to low. Cover. Simmer for 1 hour, stirring occasionally.

Add next 4 ingredients. Cover. Simmer for about 45 minutes, stirring occasionally, until beef and yam are tender.

Add peanut butter and spinach. Stir. Heat and stir for 2 to 3 minutes until combined and spinach is wilted. Makes 6 cups (1.5 L). Serves 6.

1 serving: 531 Calories; 25.9 g Total Fat (11.5 g Mono, 4.2 g Poly, 7.8 g Sat); 83 mg Cholesterol; 37 g Carbohydrate; 5 g Fibre; 40 g Protein; 662 mg Sodium

Pictured on page 35.

Top: Swiss Stew, page 33
Bottom: Beef And Yam Stew, above

The perfect dish to serve at your next barbecue.

note

Only 15 minutes to assemble.

time saver

Start the bamboo skewers soaking before preparing the marinade.

Beef Kabobs With Oregano And Onion

RED WINE MARINADE

Olive (or cooking) oil	1/3 cup	75 mL
Dry red (or alcohol-free) wine	1/3 cup	75 mL
Red wine vinegar	1/4 cup	60 mL
Dried whole oregano	1 tbsp.	15 mL
Garlic clove, minced (or 1/4 tsp., 1 mL, powder)	1	1
Salt	1 tsp.	5 mL
Hot pepper sauce, dash		
Beef inside round (or sirloin tip) steak, cut into twenty 1 inch (2.5 cm) cubes	1 lb.	454 g
Pickled onions	15	15
Whole fresh mushrooms	15	15
Red medium peppers, cut into fifteen 2 inch (5 cm) chunks	2	2
Bamboo skewers (12 inch, 30 cm, length), soaked in water for 10 minutes	5	5

Red Wine Marinade: Combine first 7 ingredients in shallow dish.

Add beef. Stir until coated. Cover. Marinate in refrigerator for at least 6 hours or overnight, stirring several times. Let stand at room temperature for 1 hour before barbecuing. Drain, reserving marinade. Boil marinade in small saucepan for 5 minutes.

Alternate beef, onions, mushrooms and red peppers on skewers. Brush with reserved marinade. Preheat gas barbecue to medium. Place skewers on greased grill. Cook for 6 to 8 minutes, turning and basting often, until desired doneness. Discard any remaining marinade. Makes 5 kabobs.

1 kabob: 232 Calories; 7.2 g Total Fat (14.4 g Mono, 1.9 g Poly, 4 g Sat); 53 mg Cholesterol; 12 g Carbohydrate; 1 g Fibre; 21 g Protein; 879 mg Sodium

Pictured on page 37.

Top Left: Bulgogi, page 38
Top Right: Beef Kabobs With Oregano And Onion, above
Bottom: Sesame Kabobs With Spinach, page 39

Bohl-GOH-gee, Korean barbecued beef, is one of the most familiar and loved recipes in Korean restaurants. Now it can be a big hit at your house.

notes

To toast sesame seeds, place in single layer in ungreased shallow pan. Bake in 350°F (175°C) oven for 5 to 10 minutes, stirring or shaking often, until desired doneness.

Use partially frozen steak for easy slicing.

time saver

Start the bamboo skewers soaking before preparing the marinade.

serving suggestion

Serve with peanut sauce and rice.

Bulgogi

MARINADE

Soy sauce	1/3 cup	75 mL
Brown sugar, packed	3 tbsp.	50 mL
Dry sherry	2 tbsp.	30 mL
Green onions, sliced	3	3
Garlic cloves, chopped (or 1 tsp., 5 mL, powder)	4	4
Cayenne pepper	1/4 tsp.	1 mL
Sesame (or cooking) oil	1 tbsp.	15 mL
Sesame seeds, toasted (see Note)	1 tbsp.	15 mL
Freshly ground pepper, sprinkle		
Beef flank steak, cut across grain into paper-thin slices (see Note)	2 lbs.	900 g
Bamboo skewers (8 inch, 20 cm, length), soaked in water for 10 minutes	8	8

Marinade: Process first 9 ingredients in blender or food processor until smooth.

Place beef in shallow dish. Pour marinade over beef. Stir until coated. Cover. Marinate in refrigerator for at least 2 hours to blend flavours.

Thread beef, accordion-style, onto skewers. Preheat electric grill for 5 minutes or gas barbecue to medium. Place skewers on greased grill. Cook for about 8 minutes, turning several times, until desired doneness. Serves 8.

1 serving: 250 Calories; 12.3 g Total Fat (5 g Mono, 1.4 g Poly, 4.6 g Sat); 48 mg Cholesterol; 7 g Carbohydrate; trace Fibre; 26 g Protein; 794 mg Sodium

Pictured on page 37.

Sesame Kabobs With Spinach

GINGER MARINADE

Soy sauce	1/3 cup	75 mL
Sesame oil	1/3 cup	75 mL
Sesame seeds	2 tbsp.	30 mL
Finely grated peeled gingerroot (or 1 1/2 tsp., 7 mL, ground ginger)	2 tbsp.	30 mL
Beef inside round (or sirloin tip) steak, cut into sixteen 1 inch (2.5 cm) cubes	1 lb.	454 g
Large red onion, cut into 16 wedges	1	1
Large yellow pepper, cut into sixteen 1 inch (2.5 cm) pieces	1	1
Large orange pepper, cut into sixteen 1 inch (2.5 cm) pieces	1	1
Bamboo skewers (10 inch, 25 cm, length), soaked in water for 10 minutes	8	8
Bag of fresh spinach, stems removed	10 oz.	285 g
Large tomato, cut into wedges	1	1

Ginger Marinade: Combine first 4 ingredients in shallow dish. Reserve 1/4 cup (60 mL) marinade.

Add beef to remaining marinade. Stir until coated. Cover. Marinate in refrigerator for at least 2 hours to blend flavours. Drain, reserving marinade. Boil marinade in small saucepan for 5 minutes.

Alternate beef, onion, yellow pepper and orange pepper on skewers. Brush with marinade. Discard any remaining marinade. Place skewers on broiler pan rack.

Combine spinach, tomato and first amount of reserved marinade in bottom of broiler pan. Place rack of skewers on top. Broil on second rack from top in oven for 12 to 15 minutes for medium-rare or until desired doneness, turning once. Drain spinach and tomato. Place on warmed platter. Lay kabobs on spinach mixture. Serve immediately. Makes 8 kabobs with 2 cups (500 mL) spinach mixture.

1 kabob plus 1/4 cup (60 mL) spinach mixture: 128 Calories; 6.3 g Total Fat (2.5 g Mono, 1.9 g Poly, 1.4 g Sat); 27 mg Cholesterol; 5 g Carbohydrate; 2 g Fibre; 13 g Protein; 325 mg Sodium

Pictured on page 37.

Tender and flavourful chunks of beef and peppers laid over a bed of spinach. Sesame oil is more expensive but well worth having on hand for other Asian-type recipes.

time saver

Start the bamboo skewers soaking before preparing the marinade.

serving suggestion

Serve with rice for a full meal.

These spicy ribs will be a hit.

serving suggestion

Serve remaining sauce over rice or mashed potatoes.

Barbecued Beef Ribs

Beef back ribs, cut into serving-size pieces	4 lbs.	1.8 kg
Water	3 tbsp.	50 mL
Freshly ground pepper, sprinkle		
BARBECUE SAUCE		
Can of tomato sauce	7 1/2 oz.	213 mL
Chili sauce	1 cup	250 mL
Dijon mustard	2 tbsp.	30 mL
Lemon juice	1 tbsp.	15 mL
Garlic cloves, minced (or 1/2 tsp., 2 mL, powder)	2	2
Brown sugar, packed	1 tsp.	5 mL
Hot pepper sauce	1 tsp.	5 mL
Dried crushed chilies	1 tsp.	5 mL

Divide ribs between 2 large sheets of heavy-duty (or double layer of regular) foil. Sprinkle with water and pepper. Bring long sides of foil up over ribs and fold together. Crease to seal top. Press short sides of foil together at each end. Fold to seal each packet well. Preheat gas barbecue to low. Place packets on grill. Cook for 1 1/2 hours, turning every 20 minutes.

Barbecue Sauce: Combine all 8 ingredients in medium saucepan. Bring to a boil. Reduce heat. Simmer, uncovered, for 10 to 15 minutes until slightly reduced and thickened. Makes about 2 cups (500 mL) sauce. Remove ribs from foil. Place directly on greased grill over medium heat. Brush ribs well with sauce. Cook for 10 minutes, turning and basting once, until browned and glazed. Serves 6.

1 serving: 606 Calories; 40.1 g Total Fat (16.8 g Mono, 1.7 g Poly, 16.2 g Sat); 115 g Cholesterol; 16 g Carbohydrate; 3 g Fiber; 44 g Protein; 1036 mg Sodium

Pictured on page 41.

Who would have thought you could make company fare from plain short ribs?

note

If you have a hard time finding short ribs, use same amount of side ribs, separated into single ribs, and baked for 3 to 4 hours.

Short Ribs

Beef short ribs, bone-in (see Note)	4 lbs.	1.8 kg
RIB SAUCE		
Can of tomato sauce	7 1/2 oz.	213 mL
Fancy mild molasses	2 tbsp.	30 mL
White vinegar	2 tbsp.	30 mL
Dry onion flakes	1 tbsp.	15 mL
Salt	1 1/2 tsp.	7 mL
Pepper	1/2 tsp.	2 mL

Place ribs in ungreased 4 quart (4 L) casserole or medium roaster.

Rib Sauce: Combine all 6 ingredients in small bowl. Pour over ribs. Cover. Bake in 300°F (150°C) oven for 4 to 5 hours until tender. Remove ribs to serving bowl. Tip pan slightly to skim fat off sauce. Spoon sauce over ribs. Serves 6.

1 serving: 300 Calories; 15.7 g Total Fat (6.9 g Mono, 0.5 g Poly, 6.7 g Sat); 74 mg Cholesterol; 8 g Carbohydrate; 1 g Fibre; 30 g Protein; 960 mg Sodium

Pictured below.

Company Meatloaf

Finely chopped onion	1 1/4 cups	300 mL
Fine dry bread crumbs	1 cup	250 mL
Grated sharp Cheddar cheese	1 cup	250 mL
Milk	2/3 cup	150 mL
Grated carrot	2/3 cup	150 mL
Large eggs, fork-beaten	2	2
Seasoning salt	1 tsp.	5 mL
Worcestershire sauce	1 tsp.	5 mL
Salt	1 tsp.	5 mL
Pepper	1/4 tsp.	1 mL
Lean ground beef	1 1/2 lbs.	680 g
Ketchup	1/4 cup	60 mL
Brown sugar, packed	1/4 cup	60 mL
Prepared mustard	2 tsp.	10 mL

Fairly traditional meatloaf, but with a "crowning" touch.

time saver

Prepare the meatloaf in the morning and have ready in the pan, or make ahead, without the glaze, and freeze.

Combine first 10 ingredients in large bowl. Stir. Let stand for about 5 minutes until bread crumbs are moistened.

Add ground beef. Mix well. Turn into greased 9 x 5 x 3 inch (22 x 12.5 x 7.5 cm) loaf pan. Bake in 350°F (175°C) oven for 1 hour. Drain.

Combine ketchup, brown sugar and mustard in small bowl. Spread over top of meatloaf. Bake in 350°F (175°C) oven for about 30 minutes until no longer pink inside. Drain off any remaining fat. Cuts into 8 slices.

1 slice: 329 Calories; 14.3 g Total Fat (5.3 g Mono, 0.9 g Poly, 6.6 g Sat); 114 mg Cholesterol; 26 g Carbohydrate; 1 g Fibre; 24 g Protein; 909 mg Sodium

Pictured below.

A tunnel of creamy mushroom filling encased in meatloaf walls.

Mushroom-Stuffed Meatloaf

FILLING

Hard margarine (or butter)	1 tbsp.	15 mL
Chopped fresh mushrooms	3 cups	750 mL
Chopped onion	1 cup	250 mL
All-purpose flour	3 tbsp.	50 mL
Dried thyme	1/2 tsp.	2 mL
Salt	1/2 tsp.	2 mL
Pepper	1/4 tsp.	1 mL
Block of cream cheese, cut up	4 oz.	125 g

MEAT LAYER

Fine dry bread crumbs	2/3 cup	150 mL
Milk	1/4 cup	60 mL
Large egg, fork-beaten	1	1
Soy sauce	3 tbsp.	50 mL
Ground ginger	1/2 tsp.	2 mL
Worcestershire sauce	1/2 tsp.	2 mL
Garlic powder	1/4 tsp.	1 mL
Lean ground beef	1 1/2 lbs.	680 g

Filling: Melt margarine in frying pan on medium. Add mushrooms and onion. Cook for 5 to 10 minutes, stirring often, until onion is softened and liquid from mushrooms is evaporated. Reduce heat to medium.

Add flour, thyme, salt and pepper. Stir quickly until well-combined. Add cream cheese. Stir until blended. Cool.

Meat Layer: Combine first 7 ingredients in large bowl.

Add ground beef. Mix well. Place about 2/3 of beef mixture in greased 9 x 5 x 3 inch (22 x 12.5 x 7.5 cm) loaf pan. Pack mixture into bottom and 2 inches (5 cm) up sides of pan. Spoon mushroom mixture into cavity. Spread evenly. Flatten remaining 1/3 of beef mixture. Place on top, smoothing and sealing sides. Bake, uncovered, in 325°F (160°C) oven for about 1 hour until browned. Serves 6.

1 serving: 444 Calories; 28.2 g Total Fat (11.4 g Mono, 1.6 g Poly, 12.3 g Sat); 123 mg Cholesterol; 19 g Carbohydrate; 2 g Fibre; 28 g Protein; 1012 mg Sodium

Pictured on page 45.

note

To freeze large quantities of meatballs ahead of time, arrange cooked and drained meatballs in single layer on baking sheet. Freeze, uncovered, for about 1 hour until firm. Place in airtight container. Freeze for up to 2 months.

variation

These are also wonderful served as an appetizer. Shape into 1 inch (2.5 cm) balls. Makes 68 meatballs.

You might also want to try the scrumptious sweet garlic sauce as a dip.

Honey Garlic Meatballs

MEATBALLS

Lean ground beef	2 lbs.	900 g
Fresh white bread slices, processed into crumbs	4	4
Large eggs, fork-beaten	2	2
Salt	1 tsp.	5 mL
Cayenne pepper	1/4 tsp.	1 mL

HONEY GARLIC SAUCE

Hard margarine (or butter)	1 tbsp.	15 mL
Garlic cloves, minced	8	8
Can of stewed tomatoes (with juice), puréed	14 oz.	398 mL
Liquid honey	3/4 cup	175 mL
Soy sauce	1/4 cup	60 mL
Cornstarch	2 tsp.	10 mL

Meatballs: Combine all 5 ingredients in large bowl. Mix well. Shape into 1 1/2 inch (3.8 cm) balls. Arrange in single layer on ungreased baking sheet. Bake in 500°F (260°C) oven for 10 to 12 minutes until browned. Transfer to ungreased 2 quart (2 L) casserole.

Honey Garlic Sauce: Melt margarine in medium saucepan on medium. Add garlic. Heat and stir until garlic is soft but not browned.

Add tomatoes and honey. Stir.

Stir soy sauce into cornstarch in small bowl until smooth. Stir into tomato mixture. Bring to a boil, stirring constantly, until slightly thickened. Makes about 2 1/4 cups (550 mL) sauce. Pour sauce over meatballs. Bake, uncovered, in 350°F (175°C) oven for about 20 minutes until meatballs are glazed. Serves 8.

1 serving: 354 Calories; 12.6 g Total Fat (5.7 g Mono, 0.9 g Poly, 4.5 g Sat); 112 mg Cholesterol; 37 g Carbohydrate; trace Fibre; 24 g Protein; 1132 mg Sodium

Pictured on page 47.

Top: Tourtière Québécoise, page 48
Bottom: Honey Garlic Meatballs, above

Thanks to the French Canadians for this great meat pie. It's so good you'll want to freeze some to keep on hand.

note

Mashed potatoes should be smooth and free from lumps for best results.

Tourtière Québécoise

Lean ground beef	1 lb.	454 g
Lean ground pork	1/2 lb.	225 g
Finely chopped onion	1 cup	250 mL
Ground cinnamon	3/4 tsp.	4 mL
Garlic powder	1/4 tsp.	1 mL
Ground cloves	1/8 tsp.	0.5 mL
Salt	1 tsp.	5 mL
Pepper	1/4 tsp.	1 mL
Mashed potatoes (see Note)	1 cup	250 mL
Pastry for 2 crust pie, your own or a mix	1	1
Large egg, fork-beaten (optional)	1	1

Combine first 8 ingredients in large pot or Dutch oven. Bring to a boil, stirring often. Simmer, uncovered, stirring occasionally, for about 15 minutes until beef and pork are no longer pink.

Add potatoes. Mixture should be moist and thick. Cool thoroughly.

Divide pastry into 2 balls, 1 larger than the other. Roll out larger ball on lightly floured surface to fit 9 inch (22 cm) pie plate. Turn beef mixture into pie shell. Roll out remaining pastry to fit top. Dampen edge of bottom crust. Cover with top pastry. Trim and crimp edge to seal. Brush with egg. Cut small slits in top to allow steam to escape. Bake in 350°F (175°C) oven for about 45 minutes until browned. Cuts into 6 wedges.

1 wedge: 400 Calories; 25 g Total Fat (11.3 g Mono, 2.2 g Poly, 9 g Sat); 52 mg Cholesterol; 25 g Carbohydrate; trace Fibre; 18 g Protein; 557 mg Sodium

Pictured on page 47.

No-Fuss Stroganoff

Hard margarine (or butter)	2 tbsp.	30 mL
Finely chopped onion	1 cup	250 mL
Lean ground beef	1 lb.	454 g
All-purpose flour	2 tbsp.	30 mL
Salt	1 tsp.	5 mL
Pepper	1/4 tsp.	1 mL
Can of mushroom stems and pieces, drained	10 oz.	284 mL
Can of condensed cream of chicken soup	10 oz.	284 mL
Sour cream	1/2 cup	125 mL
Grated medium Cheddar cheese	1/4 cup	60 mL

Melt margarine in large frying pan on medium. Add onion. Cook for 5 to 10 minutes, stirring often, until softened. Add ground beef. Scramble-fry until no longer pink. Drain.

Sprinkle flour, salt and pepper over beef mixture. Stir. Add mushrooms. Cook for 10 minutes, stirring occasionally.

Add soup. Cook and stir for about 10 minutes, until heated through.

Add sour cream and cheese. Heat and stir until cheese is melted. Serves 4.

1 serving: 377 Calories; 23 g Total Fat (8.7 g Mono, 1.6 g Poly, 10.6 g Sat); 88 mg Cholesterol; 15 g Carbohydrate; 2 g Fibre; 27 g Protein; 1536 mg Sodium

Pictured on page 51.

A really delicious gourmet casserole using ground beef.

note

Serve immediately or pour into a casserole, cover, and keep in warm oven.

serving suggestion

Serve over broad egg noodles.

This classic French dish is always a hit.

serving suggestion

Serve with steamed green beans and red peppers.

Veal Cutlets In Wine Sauce

Hard margarine (butter browns too fast)	2 tbsp.	30 mL
Veal cutlets (about 4 oz., 113 g, each)	8	8
Salt, sprinkle		
Pepper, sprinkle		

WINE SAUCE

Hard margarine (or butter)	1/4 cup	60 mL
All-purpose flour	1/4 cup	60 mL
Salt	1/2 tsp.	2 mL
Pepper	1/16 tsp.	0.5 mL
Beef bouillon powder	1 tbsp.	15 mL
Milk	2 cups	500 mL
Dry white (or alcohol-free) wine	1/4 cup	60 mL

Melt margarine in frying pan on medium. Add veal. Cook for about 4 minutes per side until desired doneness. Add more margarine if needed. Sprinkle with salt and pepper. Transfer to plate. Cover to keep warm.

Wine Sauce: Melt margarine in same frying pan on medium. Stir in flour, salt, pepper and bouillon powder until smooth. Gradually stir in milk and wine until boiling and thickened. Makes 2 1/2 cups (625 mL) sauce. Spoon 2 tbsp. (30 mL) sauce onto centre of 8 warm dinner plates. Place veal on top. Divide and spoon remaining sauce over top. Serves 8.

1 serving: 254 Calories; 11.6 g Total Fat (4.5 g Mono, 1 g Poly, 5.5 g Sat); 125 mg Cholesterol; 7 g Carbohydrate; trace Fibre; 28 g Protein; 548 mg Sodium

Pictured on page 51.

Top: No-Fuss Stroganoff, page 49
Bottom: Veal Cutlets In Wine Sauce, above

Practically no work to this and yet it makes for a special evening meal. Easy to double or triple for several guests.

time saver

Prepare sauce and spread over salmon. Cover. Chill for up to 4 hours until ready to cook.

note

To transfer salmon in foil easily to barbecue, place on baking sheet, then slide onto grill.

serving suggestion

Serve with rice, fresh asparagus and lemon wedge.

Salmon 'Chanted Evening

Salmon fillet (with skin)	4 lbs.	1.8 kg
Salad dressing (such as Miracle Whip)	1/2 cup	125 mL
Ketchup	1/4 cup	60 mL
Brown sugar, packed	1/4 cup	60 mL
Lemon juice	2 tbsp.	30 mL
Parsley flakes	1 tsp.	5 mL
Worcestershire sauce	1/2 tsp.	2 mL
Salt	1/2 tsp.	2 mL
Pepper	1/8 tsp.	0.5 mL

Place salmon, skin-side down, on greased heavy-duty (or double layer of regular) foil, large enough to cover top loosely. Pat top of salmon dry with paper towel.

Combine remaining 8 ingredients in small bowl. Stir well. Spread over top of salmon. Preheat gas barbecue to medium-high. Place salmon in foil on grill. Using skewer, poke holes, at 2 inch (5cm) intervals, through salmon right down through foil as well. Bring foil up over ends of salmon to cover loosely. Leave sides exposed. Close lid. Cook for about 20 minutes until salmon flakes easily when tested with fork. Allow 10 minutes per 1 inch (2.5 cm) thickness plus 5 minutes for foil. Makes twelve 5 oz. (140 g) servings.

1 serving: 291 Calories; 14.7 g Total Fat (6 g Mono, 5.5 g Poly, 1.9 g Sat); 86 mg Cholesterol; 8 g Carbohydrate; trace Fibre; 30 g Protein; 298 mg Sodium

Pictured on page 53.

Broiled Salmon

A very mild sauce is brushed over steaks before broiling.

serving suggestion

Serve with your favourite salad.

Hard margarine (or butter)	3 tbsp.	50 mL
Lemon juice	1 tbsp.	15 mL
Parsley flakes	1/4 tsp.	1 mL
Onion salt	1/4 tsp.	1 mL
Salt	1/4 tsp.	1 mL
Paprika	1/8 tsp.	0.5 mL
Dried tarragon leaves	1/8 tsp.	0.5 mL
Salmon steaks (about 4 oz., 113 g, each)	2	2

Combine first 7 ingredients in small saucepan. Heat and stir on medium until margarine is melted.

Place salmon on greased rack in broiler pan. Brush with lemon mixture. Broil on second rack from top in oven for about 8 minutes until browned. Turn carefully. Brush with lemon mixture. Broil for about 5 minutes until salmon flakes easily when tested with fork. Serves 2.

1 serving: 371 Calories; 27.1 g Total Fat (8.2 g Mono, 4.5 g Poly, 12.4 g Sat); 130 mg Cholesterol; 1 g Carbohydrate; trace Fibre; 30 Protein; 696 mg Sodium

Pictured on page 55.

Orange And Dill Salmon

Salmon steaks marinated in citrus juice, maple syrup, wine and dill. Barbecued to perfection.

serving suggestion

Serve with grilled vegetables and orange wedges.

Orange juice	1/2 cup	125 mL
Maple (or maple-flavoured) syrup	1/3 cup	75 mL
Dry white (or alcohol-free) wine	1/4 cup	60 mL
Chopped fresh dill (or 1 tbsp., 15 mL, dill weed)	1/4 cup	60 mL
Soy sauce	1 tbsp.	15 mL
Salmon steaks (3/4 – 1 inch, 2 – 2.5 cm, thick), about 4 oz. (113 g) each	4	4

(continued on next page)

Combine first 5 ingredients in small bowl.

Place salmon in shallow dish. Pour marinade over top. Turn until coated. Cover. Marinate in refrigerator for up to 4 hours. Remove salmon. Discard marinade. Preheat electric grill for 5 minutes or gas barbecue to medium. Cook salmon on greased grill for about 5 minutes per side until salmon flakes easily when tested with fork. Serves 4.

1 serving: 209 Calories; 7.2 g Total Fat (2.4 g Mono, 2.9 g Poly, 1.1 g Sat); 62 mg Cholesterol; 11 g Carbohydrate; trace Fibre; 23 g Protein; 182 mg Sodium

Pictured below.

Top: Broiled Salmon, page 54
Bottom: Orange And Dill Salmon, page 54

A seasoned, crunchy, golden coating keeps the salmon moist as it grills to perfection.

Cornmeal-Crusted Salmon

CORNMEAL COATING

Yellow cornmeal	1/3 cup	75 mL
Onion powder	1 tsp.	5 mL
Paprika	1 tsp.	5 mL
Seasoned salt	3/4 tsp.	4 mL
Dried thyme, crushed	1/2 tsp.	2 mL
Garlic powder (optional)	1/4 tsp.	1 mL
Hard margarine (or butter)	3 tbsp.	50 mL
Lemon juice	2 tsp.	10 mL
Centre-cut salmon fillets (about 4 oz., 113 g, each), skin removed	4	4

Cornmeal Coating: Combine first 6 ingredients in shallow dish.

Melt margarine in small saucepan. Stir in lemon juice.

Pat salmon dry with paper towels. Brush both sides with margarine mixture. Roll in cornmeal mixture until coated. Preheat electric grill for 5 minutes or gas barbecue to medium. Cook salmon on greased grill for 5 to 8 minutes per side until salmon flakes easily when tested with fork. Serves 4.

1 serving: 383 Calories; 24.2 g Total Fat (11.1 g Mono, 6.5 g Poly, 4.9 g Sat); 83 mg Cholesterol; 11 g Carbohydrate; 1 g Fibre; 29 g Protein; 408 mg Sodium

Pictured on page 59.

If you have never had sea bass, this is a must-try recipe. Absolutely wonderful.

serving suggestion

Delicious served over wild rice.

Sea Bass À La Caesar

Creamy Caesar dressing	2 tbsp.	30 mL
Lemon juice	2 tsp.	10 mL
Garlic cloves, minced (or 1/2 tsp., 2 mL, powder)	2	2
Fresh sea bass steaks (about 4 oz., 113 g, each), see Note	2	2

Coarse ground pepper, generous sprinkle
Fresh oregano leaves (or marjoram sprigs), to cover surface of fish

(continued on next page)

Combine dressing, lemon juice and garlic in small bowl.

Spread over top surface of fish steaks.

Sprinkle with pepper. Lay oregano leaves over top. Preheat two-sided electric grill for 5 minutes. Place fish on lightly greased grill. Close lid. Cook for 6 to 8 minutes until fish flakes easily with fork near bone. Serves 2.

1 serving: 273 Calories; 13.6 g Total Fat (6.5 g Mono, 4.2 g Poly, 1.9 g Sat); 119 mg Cholesterol; 3 g Carbohydrate; trace Fibre; 32 g Protein; 213 mg Sodium

Pictured on page 58.

Pictured on page 58.

note

If using frozen sea bass steaks, place frozen fish on grill. Close lid. Cook for about 10 minutes until fish flakes easily near bone when tested with fork.

Just For The Halibut

Fine dry bread crumbs	1 cup	250 mL
Dry onion soup mix, stirred before measuring	2 tbsp.	30 mL
Grated Parmesan cheese	2 tbsp.	30 mL
Parsley flakes	1 tsp.	5 mL
Paprika	1/2 tsp.	2 mL
Salt	1 tsp.	5 mL
Pepper	1/4 tsp.	1 mL
Halibut fillets (about 1/3 lb., 150 g, each)	6	6
Sour cream	1 cup	250 mL
Hard margarine (or butter), melted	1/4 cup	60 mL

Combine first 7 ingredients in small bowl.

Dip fish fillets into sour cream. Roll in crumb mixture until coated. Place in well-greased shallow baking pan.

Drizzle with margarine. Bake in 500°F (260°C) oven for 10 to 12 minutes until fish flakes easily when tested with fork. Serves 6.

1 serving: 401 Calories; 19.3 g Total Fat (5.9 g Mono, 2.1 g Poly, 9.8 g Sat); 88 mg Cholesterol; 18 g Carbohydrate; 1 g Fibre; 37 g Protein; 1229 mg Sodium

Pictured on page 59.

Grated Parmesan cheese adds to the flavour of this crumbed and browned dish. The rich brown colour comes from dry onion soup.

Pictured on Next Page:
Centre Left: Sea Bass À La Caesar, page 56
Top Right: Cornmeal-Crusted Salmon, page 56
Bottom Right: Just For The Halibut, this page

Aromatic, subtly flavoured fennel with the bright addition of sun-dried tomatoes.

Fish And Fennel Parcels

Cooking oil	1 tbsp.	15 mL
Fennel bulb (white part only), thinly sliced	1	1
Garlic clove, minced (or 1/4 tsp., 1 mL, powder)	1	1
Dry white (or alcohol-free) wine	1/2 cup	125 mL
Hard margarine (or butter), melted	4 tsp.	20 mL
Finely grated orange zest	1/2 tsp.	2 mL
Salt	1/4 tsp.	1 mL
Pepper	1/4 tsp.	1 mL
Snapper fillets (about 4 oz., 113 g, each)	4	4
Sun-dried tomatoes in oil, drained and finely chopped	1/3 cup	75 mL

Heat cooking oil in large frying pan on medium-low. Add fennel and garlic. Cook for about 10 minutes, stirring often, until fennel is soft and lightly browned.

Combine next 5 ingredients in small bowl.

Lay out 4 sheets of ungreased heavy-duty (or double layer of regular) foil, about 16 inches (40 cm) long (depending on length of fillets). Divide fennel mixture among pieces of foil. Place fish on top. Drizzle with wine mixture.

Scatter tomato over fish. Bring up short sides of foil to meet over fish. Fold foil downwards several times to seal very well. Fold opposite sides in and secure firmly. Preheat gas barbecue to medium. Place packets on ungreased grill. Close lid. Cook for about 10 minutes until fish flakes easily when tested with fork. Serves 4.

1 serving: 232 Calories; 9.1 g Total Fat (4.9 g Mono, 2 g Poly, 1.4 g Sat); 42 mg Cholesterol; 8 g Carbohydrate; trace Fibre; 25 g Protein; 398 mg Sodium

Pictured on page 61.

Top: Fish And Fennel Parcels, above
Bottom: Blackened Snapper, page 62

It's hot all right! And it's so good. Cut down the amount of cayenne pepper, if you must.

Blackened Snapper

CAJUN SEASONING

Garlic powder	1 tsp.	5 mL
Onion powder	1 tsp.	5 mL
Chili powder	1 tsp.	5 mL
Paprika	1 tsp.	5 mL
Pepper	1/2 tsp.	2 mL
Cayenne pepper	1/2 tsp.	2 mL
Dried thyme	1/4 tsp.	1 mL
Snapper fillets (about 4 oz., 113 g, each)	6	6
Cooking oil	1 1/2 tbsp.	25 mL

Cajun Seasoning: Measure first 7 ingredients into shallow bowl. Stir well to mix.

Heat lightly greased frying pan (cast iron pan is best) until very hot. Pat fish dry with paper towels. Brush with cooking oil. Dip into seasoning until well-coated. Place in hot frying pan. Cook for 2 minutes. Turn. Cook for 2 to 3 minutes until fish flakes easily when tested with fork. Serves 6.

1 serving: 150 Calories; 5.1 g Total Fat (2.3 g Mono, 1.6 g Poly, 0.6 g Sat); 42 mg Cholesterol; 1 g Carbohydrate; trace Fibre; 24 g Protein; 78 mg Sodium

Pictured on page 61.

Cheesy Fish Fillets

Cod fillets (about 4 oz., 113 g, each)	4	4
Sour cream	1/4 cup	60 mL
Lemon juice	1 tbsp.	15 mL
Garlic salt	1/2 tsp.	2 mL
Dill weed	1/2 tsp.	2 mL
Grated Havarti (or Dofino) cheese	1/3 cup	75 mL

Oven-baked fish broiled briefly for a very attractive and tasty dish.

Arrange fish fillets in single layer on greased baking sheet with sides.

Combine next 4 ingredients in small bowl. Spoon over fish.

Sprinkle with cheese. Bake, uncovered, in 350°F (175°C) oven for 12 to 14 minutes until fish flakes easily when tested with fork. Broil for 2 to 3 minutes until cheese is bubbly and golden. Do not allow tops to brown too much. Serves 4.

1 serving: 152 Calories; 5.5 g Total Fat (1.4 g Mono, 0.4 g Poly, 3.1 g Sat); 65 mg Cholesterol; 1 g Carbohydrate; trace Fibre; 23 g Protein; 291 mg Sodium

Pictured below.

Rich, golden yellow sauce. Delicate curry flavour with slight chili bite. Serve over rice.

note

To shop for ripe mangoes, look for those that yield slightly to gentle pressure. The colouring will be deep red and/or rich yellow with only a blush of green at most. Medium to large mangoes are generally the best tasting. A ripe mango will smell fairly fruity at the stem end as long as it is not cold. Avoid product that is too small, too soft or wrinkled.

time saver

To thaw frozen shrimp safely and quickly, place in colander under cold running water. Do not refreeze.

serving suggestion

Serve over rice.

Shrimp Mango Curry

Hard margarine (or butter)	1 tbsp.	15 mL
Ripe medium mango, chopped (see Note)	1	1
Chopped onion	1/2 cup	125 mL
Diced celery	3/4 cup	175 mL
Garlic clove, minced (or 1/4 tsp., 1 mL, powder)	1	1
All-purpose flour	3 tbsp.	50 mL
Curry paste	1 1/2 tsp.	7 mL
Chili paste (sambal oelek)	1 tsp.	5 mL
Coconut milk	1 1/3 cups	325 mL
Dark raisins	1/2 cup	125 mL
Prepared chicken broth	2 cups	500 mL
Raw large shrimp (tails intact), peeled and deveined (see Time Saver)	1 1/2 lbs.	680 g
Salt	1/4 tsp.	1 mL
Brown sugar, packed	1 tbsp.	15 mL

Melt margarine in wok or frying pan on medium-high. Add mango, onion, celery and garlic. Cook for 5 to 10 minutes, stirring often, until onion is golden.

Add flour, curry paste and chili paste. Stir. Cook for 1 minute, stirring often.

Gradually add coconut milk, raisins and broth, stirring constantly, until boiling. Reduce heat to medium-low. Simmer, uncovered, for 5 minutes.

Add shrimp, salt and brown sugar. Stir. Cook for about 3 minutes, stirring continually, until shrimp turns pink and is curled. Do not overcook. Makes about 7 cups (1.75 L).

1 cup (250 mL): 310 Calories; 14.4 g Total Fat (2.3 g Mono, 1.3 g Poly, 9.5 g Sat); 148 mg Cholesterol; 24 g Carbohydrate; 2 g Fibre; 23 g Protein; 504 mg Sodium

Pictured on page 65.

Sweet, citrus-flavoured sauce complements the flavours of the sage and parsley in the herb crust.

note

To add flavour to meats without adding fat, use spice rubs and vinegar or citrus-based marinades instead of heavier oil-based marinades.

Herb-Crusted Pork

Ingredient	Imperial	Metric
Orange juice	1/2 cup	125 mL
Dry white (or alcohol-free) wine	1/2 cup	125 mL
Liquid honey	2 tbsp.	30 mL
Garlic cloves, minced (or 1/2 tsp., 2 mL, powder)	2	2
Pork tenderloin, trimmed of fat	1 lb.	454 g
Grainy mustard	1 1/2 tbsp.	25 mL
Chopped fresh parsley (or 3 – 3 1/2 tsp., 15 – 17 mL, flakes)	1/4 – 1/3 cup	60 – 75 mL
Chopped fresh sage (or 1 1/2 tsp., 7 mL, dried)	2 tbsp.	30 mL
Coarse ground pepper	1 tbsp.	15 mL

Combine first 4 ingredients in medium bowl.

Add pork. Turn to coat. Cover. Marinate in refrigerator for at least 4 hours or overnight, turning several times. Drain, reserving marinade.

Spread mustard over pork.

Combine parsley, sage and pepper in shallow dish. Roll pork in parsley mixture until completely coated. Spray with cooking spray. Place pork on greased wire rack on baking sheet with sides. Bake in 375°F (190°C) oven for 45 to 50 minutes until meat thermometer inserted in centre reads 155°F (68°C) or until desired doneness. Cover with foil. Let stand for 10 minutes. Internal temperature should rise to at least 160°F (70°C). Put reserved marinade into medium frying pan. Boil on medium-high for 5 to 7 minutes until slightly reduced and thickened. Cut pork into 1 inch (2.5 cm) slices. Serve sauce with pork. Serves 4.

1 serving: 211 Calories; 4.7 g Total Fat (1.9 g Mono, 0.5 g Poly, 1.5 g Sat); 67 mg Cholesterol; 16 g Carbohydrate; 1 g Fibre; 25 g Protein; 154 mg Sodium

Pictured on page 67.

The garlic loses its pungent taste and turns sweet with roasting.

Garlic-Stuffed Pork Roast

Boneless pork loin roast	3 1/2 lbs.	1.6 kg
Garlic cloves, cut in half	8	8
Pepper	3/4 tsp.	4 mL
Dried whole oregano	1/4 tsp.	1 mL
Parsley flakes	1/4 tsp.	1 mL
Dried rosemary	1/4 tsp.	1 mL
Dried thyme	1/4 tsp.	1 mL
HERB GRAVY		
Drippings		
Water, if necessary		
Water	1 cup	250 mL
All-purpose flour	2 tbsp.	30 mL

Make 16 small slits at regular intervals in surface of roast with sharp knife. Insert garlic into slits. Put into small roasting pan.

Combine next 5 ingredients in small bowl. Rub over top and sides of roast. Cover. Cook in 400°F (205°C) oven for 20 minutes. Reduce heat to 325°F (160°C). Cook for 1 1/2 to 2 hours until meat thermometer inserted in centre reads 155°F (68°C) or until desired doneness. Cover with foil. Let stand for 10 minutes. Internal temperature should rise to at least 160°F (70°C). Remove and discard garlic if desired.

Herb Gravy: Pour drippings, including fat, through sieve over 4 cup (1 L) liquid measure. Discard solids. Let drippings stand for 10 minutes until fat rises to surface. Carefully spoon off and discard fat. Add enough water to remaining drippings to make 1 cup (250 mL). Pour into small saucepan.

Stir second amount of water into flour in small bowl until smooth. Stir into drippings. Heat and stir on medium for 5 to 7 minutes until boiling and thickened. Makes 2 cups (500 mL) gravy. Serve with roast. Makes six 3 oz. (85 g) servings, with 24 oz. (680 g) left over.

One 3 oz. (85 g) serving with about 2 tbsp. (30 mL) gravy: 121 Calories; 4.5 g Total Fat (2 g Mono, 0.5 g Poly, 1.6 g Sat); 47 mg Cholesterol; 2 g Carbohydrate; trace Fibre; 17 g Protein; 42 mg Sodium

Pictured on page 69.

These are cooked indoors and yet you still enjoy a good barbecued flavour.

Wonderful served with corn on the cob, green peas and baked potatoes. You can bake the potatoes at the same time as the chops.

Use spareribs in place of chops. Very tasty.

A great marinade for chops. You'll never want to eat them any other way.

Serve with steamed broccoli, carrots and mashed potatoes.

Barbecued Flavoured Pork Chops

Bone-in pork chops (about 2 1/2 lbs., 1.1 kg), trimmed of fat	6	6
Chili sauce	3 tbsp.	50 mL
Brown sugar, packed	3 tbsp.	50 mL
White vinegar	3 tbsp.	50 mL
Water	6 tbsp.	100 mL
Dry mustard	2 tbsp.	30 mL

Arrange pork chops in single layer in ungreased 9 x 13 inch (22 x 33 cm) pan.

Combine remaining 5 ingredients in small bowl. Spoon over chops. Cover. Bake in 350°F (175°C) oven for 1 hour. Remove cover. Bake for about 15 minutes until chops are tender. Serves 6.

1 serving: 191 Calories; 6.1 g Total Fat (3 g Mono, 0.7 g Poly, 1.8 g Sat); 62 mg Cholesterol; 11 g Carbohydrate; trace Fibre; 23 g Protein; 183 mg Sodium

Pictured on page 71.

Best Pork Chops

GARLIC MARINADE

Water	1/2 cup	125 mL
Soy sauce	1/3 cup	75 mL
Cooking oil	1/4 cup	60 mL
Lemon pepper	3 tbsp.	50 mL
Garlic cloves, minced (or 1/2 tsp., 2 mL, powder)	2	2
Bone-in pork chops (about 2 1/2 lbs., 1.1 kg), trimmed of fat	6	6

Garlic Marinade: Combine first 5 ingredients in small bowl.

(continued on next page)

Place chops in shallow dish. Pour marinade over top. Turn until coated. Cover. Marinate in refrigerator for at least 45 minutes. Drain, reserving marinade. Boil marinade in small saucepan for 5 minutes. Preheat gas barbecue to medium. Place chops on greased grill. Cook for about 25 minutes, turning and brushing with marinade, until chops are tender. Serves 6.

1 serving: 265 Calories; 17.4 g Total Fat (9.2 g Mono, 3.5 g Poly, 3.6 g Sat); 62 mg Cholesterol; 2 g Carbohydrate; trace Fibre; 24 g Protein; 1014 mg Sodium

Pictured below.

Top: Barbecued Flavoured Pork Chops, page 70
Bottom: Best Pork Chops, page 70

Delicate orange flavour. The addition of prunes and oranges is colourful.

variation

This dish goes well with rice but you may want to thicken the juice. To each 1 cup (250 mL) juice, add a mixture of 1 tbsp (15 mL) each cornstarch and water. Heat and stir until boiling and thickened.

Orange Pork

Cooking oil (optional)	1 tbsp.	15 mL
Pork shoulder steak (or chops), trimmed of fat	3 lbs.	1.4 kg
Salt, sprinkle		
Pepper, sprinkle		
Orange juice	2 cups	500 mL
Orange marmalade	2 tbsp.	30 mL
Pitted dried prunes	12 – 18	12 – 18
Can of mandarin oranges, drained	10 oz.	284 mL

Heat cooking oil in frying pan on medium-high. Add pork. Cook for about 2 minutes per side until browned. Sprinkle with salt and pepper.

Add orange juice, marmalade and prunes. Stir. Cover. Simmer on medium-low for about 1 hour until tender.

Add oranges. Stir until heated through. Serves 6.

1 serving: 313 Calories; 10.1 g Total Fat (4.6 g Mono, 1.1 g Poly, 3.4 g Sat); 93 mg Cholesterol; 28 g Carbohydrate; 2 g Fibre; 28 g Protein; 111 mg Sodium

Pictured on page 73.

A delicious blend of flavours in tender ribs.

Barbecued Ribs

Cooking oil	3 tbsp.	50 mL
Pork side spareribs, cut into 3 – 4 bone portions	4 lbs.	1.8 kg
Large onion, chopped	1	1
Ketchup	1 cup	250 mL
Water	1 cup	250 mL
White vinegar	1/2 cup	125 mL
Brown sugar, packed	1/2 cup	125 mL
Worcestershire sauce	1 tsp.	5 mL
Salt	1 tsp.	5 mL

Heat cooking oil in large frying pan on medium-high. Add spareribs. Cook, in batches, for about 5 minutes, stirring often, until browned. Transfer to large roaster.

Combine remaining 7 ingredients in medium bowl. Pour evenly over spareribs. Cover. Bake in 350°F (175°C) oven for 1 1/2 hours. Remove cover. Bake for 15 to 30 minutes until tender. Serves 8.

1 serving: 552 Calories; 35.7 g Total Fat (16.2 g Mono, 4.4 g Poly, 11.9 g Sat); 117 mg Cholesterol; 25 g Carbohydrate; 1 g Fibre; 32 g Protein; 813 mg Sodium

Pictured on page 75.

Sauce has a wonderful pineapple flavour. Lots of juice to use as gravy.

serving suggestion

Serve over rice.

Polynesian Ribs

Can of crushed pineapple (with juice)	14 oz.	398 mL
All-purpose flour	1/3 cup	75 mL
Brown sugar, packed	1/4 cup	60 mL
White vinegar	1/4 cup	60 mL
Ketchup	1/4 cup	60 mL
Soy sauce	1 tbsp.	15 mL
Salt	1/2 tsp.	2 mL
Pepper	1/8 tsp.	0.5 mL
Pork side spareribs, cut into 2 bone portions	3 lbs.	1.4 kg

(continued on next page)

Measure first 8 ingredients into medium saucepan. Heat and stir on medium-high until boiling and thickened. Pour 1/3 of sauce into 3 1/2 quart (3.5 L) slow cooker.

Arrange 1/2 of spareribs over top. Pour 1/2 of remaining sauce over top, followed by remaining spareribs. Cover with remaining sauce. Cover. Cook on Low for 10 to 12 hours or on High for 5 to 6 hours until tender. Serves 6.

1 serving: 397 Calories; 20.9 g Total Fat (9.7 g Mono, 2.5 g Poly, 8.1 g Sat); 64 mg Cholesterol; 30 g Carbohydrate; 1 g Fibre; 22 g Protein; 624 mg Sodium

Pictured below.

Top Left: Barbecued Ribs, page 74
Bottom Right: Polynesian Ribs, page 74

Pleasing contrasts of subtle lemon grass, sharp chili and beautiful colours in this favourite Vietnamese dish.

Lemon Grass Pork

Rice vermicelli	8 oz.	225 g
Boiling water, to cover		
Cooking oil	1 tbsp.	15 mL
Medium onion, halved lengthwise and thinly sliced crosswise	1	1
Garlic cloves, minced (or 1/2 tsp., 2 mL, powder)	2	2
Boneless pork loin, cut into 1/2 inch (12 mm) thick slices	1 lb.	454 g
Stalk of lemon grass	1	1
Chili sauce	2 tbsp.	30 mL
Fish sauce	1 1/2 tbsp.	25 mL
Granulated sugar	1 tsp.	5 mL
Cayenne pepper, dash (optional)		
Thinly sliced green onion	2 tbsp.	30 mL
Julienned carrot	1/4 cup	60 mL
Thinly slivered red pepper	1/4 cup	60 mL
Cilantro sprigs, for garnish		

Cover vermicelli with boiling water in small bowl. Let stand for 2 minutes. Drain.

Heat wok or frying pan on medium-high until hot. Add cooking oil. Add onion and garlic. Stir-fry for 2 minutes. Transfer to medium bowl.

Add 1/2 of pork slices to hot wok. Stir-fry for 2 to 3 minutes until no longer pink. Add to onion mixture. Stir-fry remaining pork until no longer pink. Leave in wok.

Remove outer leaves and rough tops of lemon grass, leaving 3 to 4 inch (7.5 to 10 cm) root. Place on cutting surface. Press root with flat of knife. Chop finely. Add to pork in wok.

Add next 4 ingredients. Stir. Add onion mixture and any juices. Stir-fry for about 2 minutes until pork is coated and sauce is slightly thickened. Makes 3 cups (750 mL) pork mixture. Place 1 cup (250 mL) vermicelli in each of 4 individual bowls. Divide and spoon pork mixture over vermicelli.

Arrange green onion, carrot and red pepper over pork mixture. Garnish with cilantro. Serves 4.

1 serving: 511 Calories; 18.4 g Total Fat (8.4 g Mono, 2.6 g Poly, 5.2 g Sat); 72 mg Cholesterol; 57 g Carbohydrate; 2 g Fibre; 28 g Protein; 503 mg Sodium

Pictured on page 77.

This appetizing glaze is ideal for ham steaks as well as baked. Try this glaze or any of the delicious glazes suggested.

note

A ready-to-serve ham is used in this recipe. Internal temperature should read 140°F (60°C) when done. Other hams should reach an internal temperature of 160°F (70°C).

ham with cranberry

Spread whole cranberry sauce over ham before baking.

A foolproof dinner. Sauce browns ham nicely. This recipe is also easily halved to serve 8.

Baked Ham

Fully cooked ham (bone in)	7 lbs.	3.2 kg
Whole cloves		
Liquid honey	1/2 cup	125 mL
Brown sugar, packed	1 cup	250 mL

Score ham rind in diamond shape pattern about 1/4 inch (6 mm) deep with sharp knife. Put ham into large roaster. Cover. Bake in 350°F (175°C) oven for 2 hours.

Stick whole clove into each diamond shape in ham. Increase heat to 450°F (230°C).

Heat honey in small saucepan until hot. Add brown sugar. Heat and stir until smooth. Brush over ham. Bake, uncovered, for about 15 minutes, brushing once with glaze, until well-glazed. Serves 10.

1 serving: 338 Calories; 7 g Total Fat (4.3 g Mono, 1.1 g Poly, 3.2 g Sat); 104 mg Cholesterol; 42 g Carbohydrate; 0 g Fibre; 28 g Protein; 2226 mg Sodium

Pictured on page 79.

Honey Ham Steaks

HONEY MUSTARD SAUCE

Brown sugar, packed	1/2 cup	125 mL
Hard margarine (or butter)	1/2 cup	125 mL
Liquid honey	2 tbsp.	30 mL
Soy sauce	2 tsp.	10 mL
Prepared mustard	2 tsp.	10 mL
Ham steak, trimmed of fat	4 lbs.	1.8 kg

Honey Mustard Sauce: Combine first 5 ingredients in small saucepan. Heat and stir until margarine is melted and ingredients are blended. Makes about 3/4 cup (175 mL) sauce.

(continued on next page)

Preheat gas barbecue to medium-high. Place ham on greased grill. Brush 2 tbsp. (30 mL) sauce over top of ham. Cook until lightly browned. Turn. Brush with 2 tbsp. (30 mL) sauce. Cook until glazed and heated through. Do not overcook. Serve remaining sauce on side. Serves 16.

1 serving: 229 Calories; 10.9 g Total Fat (4 g Mono, 0.8 g Poly, 5.4 g Sat); 67 mg Cholesterol; 9 g Carbohydrate; trace Fibre; 22 g Protein; 1558 mg Sodium

Pictured below.

serving suggestion

Delicious served with potatoes and red peppers.

Top Left: Baked Ham, page 78
Bottom Right: Honey Ham Steaks, page 78

Slow cooking is the secret to this wonderfully tender lamb dish.

note

Sambal oelek is a multi-purpose condiment popular in Indonesia, Malaysia and Southern India. It is a blend of chilies, brown sugar and salt and is found in the Asian section of grocery stores. It helps to make this dish what it is—splendid!

Lamb Shanks In Tomato Wine Sauce

Cooking oil	1 tbsp.	15 mL
Lamb shanks, trimmed of fat	6	6
Cooking oil	1 tbsp.	15 mL
Medium onions, thinly sliced	2	2
Garlic cloves, crushed (or 1 tsp., 5 mL, powder)	4	4
Chili paste (sambal oelek, see Note)	1/2 tsp.	2 mL
Can of diced tomatoes	28 oz.	796 mL
Dry red (or alcohol-free) wine	1 cup	250 mL
Chicken broth	1/2 cup	125 mL
Tomato paste	1/4 cup	60 mL
Fresh rosemary sprigs	3	3

Heat first amount of cooking oil in large saucepan. Add lamb. Cook on medium-high for about 8 minutes, turning occasionally, until browned. Remove from saucepan to plate.

Heat second amount of cooking oil in same saucepan on medium. Add next 3 ingredients. Cook for about 5 minutes, stirring often, until onion is softened.

Add remaining 5 ingredients. Add lamb. Bring to a boil. Reduce heat to low. Cover. Cook for 1 1/2 hours. Remove lid. Simmer, uncovered, for about 30 minutes until sauce is thickened and lamb is falling off bones. Serves 4.

1 serving: 556 Calories; 33.1 g Total Fat (15 g Mono, 4.2 g Poly, 11 g Sat); 126 mg Cholesterol; 19 g Carbohydrate; 3 g Fibre; 36 g Protein; 524 mg Sodium

Pictured on page 81.

One of the most popular lamb dishes.
Be sure to start the day before.

Rack Of Lamb

MARINADE

Apple (or orange) juice	1/3 cup	75 mL
Lemon juice	1/3 cup	75 mL
White vinegar	1/4 cup	60 mL
Cooking oil	1/4 cup	60 mL
Soy sauce	2 tbsp.	30 mL
Granulated sugar	1 tbsp.	15 mL
Garlic cloves, minced (or 1/2 tsp., 2 mL, powder)	2	2
Chopped fresh chives	2 tsp.	10 mL
Dried rosemary	2 tsp.	10 mL
Racks of lamb (4 ribs each)	6	6

Marinade: Combine first 9 ingredients in small bowl.

Make a few slits in fat of each lamb rack. Place lamb in large shallow dish. (You
may have to use 2 dishes to accommodate all racks). Pour marinade over lamb.
Turn until coated. Cover. Marinate in refrigerator for at least 6 hours or
overnight. Drain, reserving marinade. Boil marinade in small saucepan for
5 minutes. Wrap each rack in greased heavy-duty (or double thickness of
regular) foil. Preheat gas barbecue to medium-high. Place wrapped lamb, meaty
side down, on grill. Cook for 15 minutes. Turn. Cook for 8 minutes. Remove foil.
Cook for 10 to 15 minutes, turning and basting often with marinade, until
tender. Serves 6.

1 serving: 568 Calories; 47.1 g Total Fat (21 g Mono, 5.9 g Poly, 16.7 g Sat); 125 mg Cholesterol;
7 g Carbohydrate; trace Fibre; 29 g Protein; 445 mg Sodium

Pictured on page 83.

Serve with fresh mint to complement
the lamb chops perfectly.

Lamb Chops

Cooking oil	2 tbsp.	30 mL
Red wine vinegar	4 tsp.	20 mL
Lemon juice	2 tsp.	10 mL
Prepared mustard	1 tsp.	5 mL
Dried rosemary	1/2 tsp.	2 mL
Onion powder	1/4 tsp.	1 mL

(continued on next page)

Lamb chops (1 inch, 2.5 cm, thick), trimmed of fat	12	12

Combine first 6 ingredients in small bowl.

Brush sauce over chops. Let stand for 15 minutes. Preheat gas barbecue to medium-high. Place chops on greased grill. Cook for about 7 minutes per side, basting often with sauce, until tender. Serves 6.

1 serving: 242 Calories; 13.6 g Total Fat (6.7 g Mono, 2 g Poly, 3.5 g Sat); 87 mg Cholesterol; 1 g Carbohydrate; trace Fibre; 28 g Protein; 90 mg Sodium

Pictured below.

Bottom Left: Rack Of Lamb, page 82
Top Right: Lamb Chops, page 82

There should be a plump chicken on your table every so often.

apple stuffing

Add 2 coarsely grated apples to No-Fuss Stuffing.

bread stuffing

Omit onion flakes. Sauté 1/2 cup (125 mL) each chopped onion and celery in 1/4 cup (60 mL) hard margarine (or butter). Mix with rest of stuffing ingredients.

sausage stuffing

Add 1/2 to 1 lb. (225 to 454 g) sausage meat, scramble-fried, to Bread Stuffing.

Roast Chicken

Whole roasting chicken	6 lbs.	2.7 kg
NO-FUSS STUFFING		
Course dry bread crumbs	6 cups	1.5 L
Dry onion flakes	1/4 cup	60 mL
Parsley flakes	1 tbsp.	15 mL
Poultry seasoning	2 tsp.	10 mL
Celery salt	1/2 tsp.	2 mL
Salt	1 tsp.	5 mL
Pepper	1/4 tsp.	1 mL
Hard margarine (or butter), melted	1/4 cup	60 mL
Water, approximately	1 1/2 cups	375 mL
CHICKEN GRAVY		
Chicken fat (or cooking oil), skimmed from drippings	1/2 cup	125 mL
All-purpose flour	1/2 cup	125 mL
Salt	1 tsp.	5 mL
Pepper	1/4 tsp.	1 mL
Drippings, plus water to make	4 cups	1 L

Tie wings close to chicken body with butcher's string.

No-Fuss Stuffing: Combine first 7 ingredients in large bowl.

Add margarine and water. Stir. Mix well. Add a bit more water, if needed, until stuffing is moist and holds together when squeezed. Loosely fill body cavity of chicken with stuffing. Secure with wooden picks or small metal skewers. Tie legs to tail. Transfer to medium roaster. Cover. Cook in 400°F (205°C) oven for 20 minutes. Reduce heat to 325°F (160°C). Cook for 2 to 2 1/2 hours until tender and meat thermometer reads 180°F (82°C). Remove cover for last few minutes of cooking to brown more, if needed. Remove stuffing. Let stand, tented with foil, for 10 minutes before carving. If you prefer to cook uncovered, be sure to baste often.

Chicken Gravy: Stir chicken fat into flour, salt and pepper in medium saucepan until smooth. Add drippings and water. Heat and stir on medium until boiling and thickened. Makes 4 cups (1 L) gravy. Serve with chicken. Serves 8.

1 serving: 928 Calories; 45.8 g Total Fat (18 g Mono, 9.1 g Poly, 14.9 g Sat); 190 mg Cholesterol; 70 g Carbohydrate; 4 g Fibre; 55 g Protein; 1631 mg Sodium

Pictured on page 85.

Butterflying the bird ensures that the meat cooks evenly and quickly. Once you taste how good chicken is prepared in this fashion, you may never barbecue it any other way!

serving suggestion

Serve with potato salad and fresh red pepper slices.

Butterflied Chicken

Whole roasting chicken	4 lbs.	1.8 kg
Hard margarine (or butter), softened	2 tbsp.	30 mL
Chopped fresh parsley (or 1 1/2 tsp., 7 mL, flakes)	2 tbsp.	30 mL
Chopped fresh sweet basil (or 1 1/2 tsp., 7 mL, dried)	2 tbsp.	30 mL
Grainy mustard	1 tbsp.	15 mL
Salt	1/2 tsp.	2 mL
Coarse ground pepper	1/2 tsp.	2 mL

Place chicken, breast-side down, on cutting board. Cut down both sides of backbone with kitchen shears or sharp knife to remove. Turn chicken, breast-side up. Press out flat.

Combine remaining 6 ingredients in small bowl. Carefully loosen, but do not remove skin. Stuff margarine mixture between meat and skin, spreading mixture as evenly as possible. Preheat gas barbecue to medium. Turn off centre or left burner. Carefully place chicken, breast-side down, on greased grill over drip pan on unlit side. Close lid. Cook for 45 minutes. Turn chicken. Cook for 40 to 45 minutes until meat thermometer inserted in breast reads 180°F (82°C). Cut into serving-size pieces. Serves 4 to 6.

1 serving: 483 Calories; 30.3 g Total Fat (13.3 g Mono, 6 g Poly, 8 g Sat); 157 mg Cholesterol; 1 g Carbohydrate; trace Fibre; 49 g Protein; 564 mg Sodium

Pictured on page 87.

Gourmet-style chicken, yet easy to do and so attractive to serve.

serving suggestion

Serve with fresh green beans tossed in sesame seeds.

Stuffed Breasts Of Chicken

STUFFING

Hard margarine (or butter)	2 tbsp.	30 mL
Finely chopped onion	2 tbsp.	30 mL
Finely chopped celery	2 tbsp.	30 mL
Coarse dry bread crumbs	1 cup	250 mL
Dried chives	1 tbsp.	15 mL
Poultry seasoning	1/4 tsp.	1 mL
Salt	1/16 tsp.	0.5 mL
Pepper, sprinkle		
Milk, approximately	1 1/2 tbsp.	25 mL
Boneless, skinless chicken breast halves (about 4 oz., 113 g, each)	4	4

MARMALADE ORANGE SAUCE

Orange marmalade	1/2 cup	125 mL
Frozen concentrated orange juice	1 tbsp.	15 mL

Stuffing: Melt margarine in medium saucepan or frying pan on medium. Add onion and celery. Cook for 5 to 10 minutes, stirring often, until onion is softened. Remove from heat.

Add next 6 ingredients. Stir well. Add more milk, if needed, until stuffing is moist and holds together when squeezed.

Pound chicken with mallet to 1/4 inch (6 mm) thickness. Divide and spoon stuffing on half of each piece. Fold over crosswise to cover stuffing. Secure with wooden picks. Transfer to 1 1/2 quart (1.5 L) dish.

Marmalade Orange Sauce: Heat marmalade and concentrated orange juice in small saucepan on low, stirring often, until smooth. Spoon some over chicken. Bake, uncovered, in 325°F (160°C) oven for about 45 minutes until tender. Cut into 1/2 inch (12 mm) slices. Arrange on individual plates. Spoon more sauce over top. Serves 4.

1 serving: 359 Calories; 8.7 g Total Fat (2.6 g Mono, 0.9 g Poly, 4.4 g Sat); 57 mg Cholesterol; 51 g Carbohydrate; 1 g Fibre; 20 g Protein; 374 mg Sodium

Pictured on page 89.

Chicken Parmesan

Ingredient	Imperial	Metric
Grated Parmesan cheese	3/4 cup	175 mL
Fine dry bread crumbs	1/2 cup	125 mL
Dried whole oregano (optional)	1/2 tsp.	2 mL
Garlic powder	1/4 tsp.	1 mL
Salt	1 tsp.	5 mL
Pepper	1/4 tsp.	1 mL
Bone-in chicken parts (see Note)	3 lbs.	1.4 kg
Hard margarine (or butter), melted	1/2 cup	125 mL

Combine first 6 ingredients in small bowl.

Dip each chicken part into melted margarine. Roll in crumb mixture until coated. Arrange in single layer in greased 9 x 13 inch (22 x 33 cm) baking pan. Cover. Bake in 350°F (175°C) oven for 1 to 1 1/4 hours until tender. Serves 4 to 6.

1 serving: 646 Calories; 41.6 g Total Fat (16.5 g Mono, 7.8 g Poly, 14 g Sat); 189 mg Cholesterol; 11 g Carbohydrate; trace Fibre; 53 g Protein; 1248 mg Sodium

Pictured below.

Tasty and quick to prepare. The addition of oregano gives a faint comparison to the flavour of pizza.

note

If desired, remove skin from chicken before dipping, to reduce fat.

Left: Stuffed Breasts Of Chicken, page 88
Right: Chicken Parmesan, this page

This dish has such a wonderful flavour and aroma, you'll want to make it again and again.

note

If desired, thicken sauce with mixture of 1 1/2 tbsp. (25 mL) cornstarch and 3 tbsp. (50 mL) water. Boil gently, stirring constantly, until thickened.

time saver

Prepare sauce ahead of time and chill until ready to bake chicken.

serving suggestion

Serve extra sauce over mashed potatoes or rice.

Margo's Rosemary Chicken

Cooking oil	2 tsp.	10 mL
Boneless, skinless chicken breast halves (about 4 oz., 113 g, each)	10	10
Water	1 cup	250 mL
Dry white (or alcohol-free) wine	1 cup	250 mL
Red wine vinegar	1/3 cup	75 mL
Ketchup	1/4 cup	60 mL
Brown sugar, packed	2 tbsp.	30 mL
Grated onion	2 tbsp.	30 mL
Cornstarch	1 tbsp.	15 mL
Dried rosemary	1 tsp.	5 mL
Dried whole oregano	1 tsp.	5 mL
Dill weed	1 tsp.	5 mL
Chicken bouillon powder	1 tsp.	5 mL
Salt	1 tsp.	5 mL
Soy sauce	1 tsp.	5 mL
Worcestershire sauce	1 tsp.	5 mL
Paprika	1/2 tsp.	2 mL
Garlic clove, minced (or 1/4 tsp., 1 mL, powder)	1	1

Heat cooking oil in non-stick frying pan on medium. Add chicken. Cook for about 4 minutes per side until browned. Transfer to ungreased 2 1/2 quart (2.5 L) casserole.

Combine remaining 16 ingredients in medium saucepan. Heat and stir on medium-high until boiling. Pour over chicken. Cover. Bake in 350°F (175°C) oven for about 1 hour until chicken is tender. Serves 10.

1 serving: 186 Calories; 2.5 g Total Fat (0.9 g Mono, 0.7 g Poly, 0.5 Sat); 68 mg Cholesterol; 6 g Carbohydrate; trace Fibre; 28 g Protein; 543 mg Sodium

Pictured on page 91.

With a little crunch from the peanut butter and some heat from the sweet chili sauce, this dish was made for the barbecue.

variation

To grill vegetables with chicken, start cooking chicken, then add vegetables if barbecue is large enough. If using smaller grill, cook chicken first, then cover to keep warm while grilling vegetables.

Sweet Heat Peanut Chicken

Crunchy peanut butter	1/3 cup	75 mL
Sweet (or regular) chili sauce	1/4 cup	60 mL
Lime juice	2 tbsp.	30 mL
Garlic cloves, crushed (or 1/2 tsp., 2 mL, powder)	2	2
Finely grated peeled gingerroot (or 1/4 tsp., 1 mL, ground ginger)	1 tsp.	5 mL
Water	3 tbsp.	50 mL
Bone-in chicken breast halves (about 4 oz., 113 g, each), skin removed	6	6

Combine first 6 ingredients in large bowl. Makes 1 cup (250 mL) sauce.

Preheat gas barbecue to medium. Add chicken to sauce. Stir until well-coated. Remove chicken from sauce. Place chicken on greased grill. Close lid. Cook for about 20 minutes, turning often, until no longer pink inside. Serves 6.

1 serving: 260 Calories; 10 g Total Fat (4.1 g Mono, 2.7 g Poly, 2.1 g Sat); 81 mg Cholesterol; 7 g Carbohydrate; 2 g Fibre; 35 g Protein; 236 mg Sodium

Pictured on page 94.

Incredibly good—the sauce is the secret.

note

To toast hazelnuts, place in single layer on ungreased shallow pan. Bake in 350°F (175°C) oven for 5 to 10 minutes, stirring or shaking often, until desired doneness.

Elegant Chicken

All-purpose flour	2 tbsp.	30 mL
Paprika	1/8 tsp.	0.5 mL
Salt	1/8 tsp.	0.5 mL
Pepper, just a pinch		
Boneless, skinless chicken breast halves (about 4 oz., 113 g, each)	4	4
Hard margarine (butter browns too fast)	1 tbsp.	15 mL
HAZELNUT SAUCE		
Sliced fresh mushrooms	1 cup	250 mL
Dry white (or alcohol-free) wine	1/2 cup	125 mL
Condensed cream of mushroom soup (1/2 of 10 oz., 284 mL, can)	2/3 cup	150 mL
Garlic powder	1/4 tsp.	1 mL
Sliced hazelnuts (filberts), toasted (see Note)	2 tbsp.	30 mL

(continued on next page)

Combine first 4 ingredients in plastic bag.

Coat chicken in flour mixture. Melt margarine in frying pan on medium. Add chicken. Cook for 8 to 10 minutes per side until no longer pink inside. Remove to serving bowl. Cover to keep warm.

Hazelnut Sauce: Put mushrooms and wine into same frying pan. Stir to loosen brown bits. Boil gently for 3 to 4 minutes until mushrooms are softened and liquid is reduced.

Add soup, garlic powder and hazelnuts. Stir. Return to a boil. Pour over chicken. Serves 4.

1 serving: 284 Calories; 10.5 g Total Fat (4.8 g Mono, 2.4 g Poly, 2.2 g Sat); 82 mg Cholesterol; 8 g Carbohydrate; trace Fibre; 33 g Protein; 419 mg Sodium

Pictured on page 95.

Chicken Mole

A MOH-lay that cooks on top of the stove.

Hard margarine (butter browns too fast)	2 tbsp.	30 mL
Boneless, skinless chicken breast halves	1 1/2 lbs.	680 g
Cans of tomato sauce (7 1/2 oz., 213 mL, each)	2	2
Medium onion, chopped	1	1
Medium green pepper, chopped	1	1
Ground almonds	1/4 cup	60 mL
Whole cloves	2	2
Chili powder	2 tsp.	10 mL
Salt	1 tsp.	5 mL
Pepper	1/4 tsp.	1 mL
Hot pepper sauce	1/4 tsp.	1 mL
Garlic powder	1/4 tsp.	1 mL
Unsweetened chocolate baking square (1 oz., 28 g), cut up	1/2	1/2

Melt margarine in frying pan on medium. Add chicken. Cook for 4 to 5 minutes per side until browned. Cut into bite-size pieces. Return to frying pan.

Add remaining 11 ingredients. Heat and stir until simmering and chocolate is melted. Reduce heat. Cover. Simmer for 30 minutes. Serves 6.

1 serving: 182 Calories; 8.2 g Total Fat (4.2 g Mono, 1.1 g Poly, 2.1 g Sat); 41 mg Cholesterol; 11 g Carbohydrate; 2 g Fibre; 18 g Protein; 902 mg Sodium

Pictured on page 94/95.

note

Spice is just right as is, but if desired, add more hot pepper sauce.

serving suggestion

Serve over rice.

Pictured on Next Page:
Left: Sweet Heat Peanut Chicken, page 92
Top Right: Elegant Chicken, page 92
Bottom Right: Chicken Mole, this page

Three choices for this classic: bake in a mushroom sauce, pan-fry, or crumb and bake.

note

To toast almonds, place in single layer in ungreased shallow pan. Bake in 350°F (175°C) oven for 5 to 10 minutes, stirring or shaking often, until desired doneness.

serving suggestion

Serve with rice and steamed carrots.

oven cordon bleu

After rolling tightly, dip bottom of chicken into melted margarine, then into fine dry bread crumbs. Put into pan. Brush with melted margarine. Sprinkle with crumbs. Cover. Bake in 350°F (175°C) oven for 45 minutes. Remove cover. Bake for about 30 minutes until golden brown.

pan condon bleu

Fry chicken rolls in margarine in frying pan until cooked through.

Chicken Cordon Bleu

Boneless, skinless chicken breast halves (about 4 oz., 113 g, each)	6	6
Salt, sprinkle		
Deli cooked ham slices (about 6 oz., 170 g)	6	6
Swiss cheese, cut into 6 sticks	6 oz.	170 g
All-purpose flour	1/4 cup	60 mL
Hard margarine (butter browns too fast)	2 tbsp.	30 mL
Chicken bouillon cubes (1/5 oz., 6 g, each)	3	3
Boiling water	1/2 cup	125 mL
Can of sliced mushrooms, drained	10 oz.	284 mL
Dry white wine (or apple juice)	1/3 cup	75 mL
All-purpose flour	2 tbsp.	30 mL
Water	1/2 cup	125 mL
Whole almonds, toasted (see Note)	1/2 cup	125 mL

Pound chicken with mallet to 1/4 inch (6 mm) thickness. Sprinkle with salt.

Lay 1 ham slice on top of 1 chicken piece. Lay cheese stick over ham. Roll up, jelly roll-style, tucking in sides. Secure with wooden picks or tie with butcher's string. Repeat with remaining ham, chicken and cheese.

Coat rolls in first amount of flour. Let stand for 20 minutes.

Melt margarine in frying pan on medium. Add rolls. Cook for about 10 minutes, turning several times, and adding more margarine as needed, until browned. Arrange in single layer in ungreased 2 quart (2 L) casserole.

Dissolve bouillon cubes in boiling water in same frying pan. Add mushrooms and wine. Pour over rolls. Cover. Bake in 350°F (175°C) oven for 1 to 1 1/2 hours until chicken is tender. Remove rolls to warm platter. Cover to keep warm.

Transfer sauce to medium saucepan. Combine second amount of flour and water in small cup until smooth. Add to sauce. Heat and stir on medium until boiling and thickened. Pour over chicken.

Garnish with almonds. Serves 6.

1 serving: 425 Calories; 23.9 g Total Fat (11.1 g Mono, 3 g Poly, 8.2 g Sat); 95 mg Cholesterol; 13 g Carbohydrate; 2 g Fibre; 37 g Protein; 1245 mg Sodium

Pictured on page 97.

A classic French chicken dish cooked in red wine.

note

To peel pearl onions, blanch quickly in boiling water, then peel.

variation

This dish may also be simmered slowly on top of stove for about same length of time.

serving suggestion

Serve with fresh tomato slices sprinkled with chopped fresh basil and crusty multi-grain bread.

Coq Au Vin

Hard margarine (butter browns too fast)	1/4 cup	60 mL
Boneless, skinless chicken breast halves (about 4 oz., 113 g, each)	8	8
Salt, sprinkle		
Pepper, sprinkle		
Chopped onion	1/2 cup	125 mL
Bacon slices, diced	6	6
Pearl onions, peeled (see Note)	12 – 20	12 – 20
Fresh small mushrooms	1/2 lb.	225 g
Garlic clove, crushed (or 1/4 tsp., 1 mL, powder)	1	1
All-purpose flour	1 tbsp.	15 mL
Dry red (or alcohol-free) wine	1 cup	250 mL
Fresh parsley sprigs	2	2
Small bay leaf	1	1
Dried thyme	1/4 tsp.	1 mL

Melt margarine in frying pan on medium. Add chicken. Cook for 4 to 5 minutes per side until browned. Sprinkle with salt and pepper. Transfer to small roaster.

Add next 5 ingredients to same frying pan. Heat and stir until bacon is crisp.

Add flour. Mix well. Stir in wine until boiling and slightly thickened.

Add parsley, bay leaf and thyme. Pour over chicken. Cover. Bake in 325°F (160°C) oven for about 1 hour until chicken is tender. Discard bay leaf. Serves 8.

1 serving: 290 Calories; 10.9 g Total Fat (5.8 g Mono, 1.5 g Poly, 2.6 g Sat); 83 mg Cholesterol; 8 g Carbohydrate; 1 g Fibre; 34 g Protein; 223 mg Sodium

Pictured on page 99.

Don't shy away from the adventurous blend of flavours in this dish. You won't believe the wonderful taste of lemon grass, pineapple and spicy curry in a creamy coconut milk sauce. A terrific special occasion taste that's great any day. It's especially good served over coconut rice.

note

Lemon grass is available in the produce section of grocery stores.

Pineapple And Coconut Chicken

Cooking oil	1 tbsp.	15 mL
Garlic cloves, crushed (or 1/2 tsp., 2 mL, powder)	2	2
Finely grated peeled gingerroot (or 1/4 tsp., 1 mL, ground ginger)	1 tsp.	5 mL
Red curry paste	2 tbsp.	30 mL
Can of coconut milk	14 oz.	398 mL
Water	1/3 cup	75 mL
Lemon grass stalk (white part only), cut in half crosswise (see Note)	1	1
Brown sugar, packed	2 tsp.	10 mL
Lime juice	2 tsp.	10 mL
Fish sauce	1 tsp.	5 mL
Salt	1/2 tsp.	2 mL
Boneless, skinless chicken breast halves, cut into cubes	1 1/2 lbs.	680 g
Can of pineapple chunks, drained	14 oz.	398 mL
Green onions, cut into 1 inch (2.5 cm) pieces	6	6

Heat cooking oil in wok or large frying pan on high. Add garlic, ginger and curry paste. Cook for 1 minute, stirring constantly, until fragrant.

Add next 7 ingredients. Simmer, uncovered, on medium for about 10 minutes until thickened. Remove and discard lemon grass.

Add chicken and pineapple. Simmer, uncovered, for 5 to 7 minutes until chicken is no longer pink.

Add green onion. Stir. Serves 6.

1 serving: 347 Calories; 20.1 g Total Fat (3.4 g Mono, 1.9 g Poly, 13 g Sat); 81 mg Cholesterol; 9 g Carbohydrate; 1 g Fibre; 33 g Protein; 267 mg Sodium

Pictured on page 101.

This recipe has a very delicate heat. Sauce has a great flavour.

Sambal oelek is a multi-purpose condiment popular in Indonesia, Malaysia and Southern India. It is a blend of chilies, brown sugar and salt and is found in the Asian section of grocery stores.

More chilies or chili paste can be added if you like it fire-alarm hot!

To wash chilies, rinse in cold water. Do not use hot water as this causes irritating fumes to rise toward your eyes and nose. Wear gloves when chopping chilies and avoid touching your eyes.

serving suggestion

Serve over noodles.

Kung Pao Chicken

KUNG PAO SAUCE

Cornstarch	1 tbsp.	15 mL
Hoisin sauce	1 tbsp.	15 mL
Soy sauce	1 tbsp.	15 mL
Chili paste (sambal oelek)	1/2 – 1 tsp.	2 – 5 mL
Water	2 tbsp.	30 mL
Soy sauce	1 tbsp.	15 mL
Cornstarch	1 tbsp.	15 mL
Boneless, skinless chicken breast halves and thighs, diced	1 lb.	454 g
Sesame (or cooking) oil	1 tsp.	5 mL
Egg white (large), fork-beaten	1	1
Garlic clove, crushed (or 1/4 tsp., 1 mL, powder)	1	1
Cooking oil	1 tbsp.	15 mL
Garlic clove, crushed (or 1/4 tsp., 1 mL, powder)	1	1
Finely grated peeled gingerroot (or 1/8 tsp., 0.5 mL, ground ginger)	1/2 tsp.	2 mL
Small carrots, thinly sliced	2	2
Diced green pepper	1/2 cup	125 mL
Diced red pepper	1/2 cup	125 mL
Fresh small red chilies, seeds and ribs removed for less heat (see Note), optional	1 – 5	1 – 5
Green onions, cut into 1 inch (2.5 cm) pieces	3	3
Cooking oil	1 tbsp.	15 mL

Kung Pao Sauce: Combine first 5 ingredients in small cup until smooth. Set aside.

Stir second amount of soy sauce into second amount of cornstarch in medium bowl until smooth.

Add next 4 ingredients. Stir until chicken is very well-coated. Set aside.

(continued on next page)

Heat wok or frying pan on medium-high until hot. Add cooking oil. Add second amount of garlic, ginger and carrot. Stir-fry for 1 minute.

Add next 4 ingredients. Stir-fry for 1 to 2 minutes until peppers are tender-crisp. Transfer to separate medium bowl.

Add second amount of cooking oil to hot wok. Add chicken mixture. Stir immediately to break up chicken pieces. Stir-fry on medium-high for about 3 minutes until chicken is no longer pink inside. Stir sauce. Stir into chicken mixture until boiling and thickened. Add pepper mixture. Heat and stir until heated through and peppers are coated. Makes 4 cups (1 L).

1 cup (250 mL): 292 Calories; 12.5 g Total Fat (6.2 g Mono, 3.8 g Poly, 1.5 g Sat); 66 mg Cholesterol; 16 g Carbohydrate; 2 g Fibre; 29 g Protein; 711 mg Sodium

Pictured below.

A thin crust pizza with lots of colour and crunch from the fresh vegetables. Although not a traditional dish in Thailand, it is North America's favourite kind of food—pizza—with a Thai kick.

notes

If you like your food spicy, add more cayenne pepper or chili-flavoured oil while cooking chicken.

To toast sesame seeds, place in single layer in ungreased shallow pan. Bake in 350°F (175°C) oven for 5 to 10 minutes, stirring or shaking often, until desired doneness.

serving suggestion

Serve with peanut sauce.

Thai Pizza On A Garlic Crust

All-purpose flour, approximately	1 1/3 cups	325 mL
Instant yeast	1 tsp.	5 mL
Salt	1/2 tsp.	2 mL
Garlic powder	1/4 tsp.	1 mL
Hot water	1/2 cup	125 mL
Cooking oil	1 tbsp.	15 mL
Peanut sauce	1/4 cup	60 mL
Grated part-skim mozzarella cheese	3/4 cup	175 mL
Cooking (or chili-flavoured) oil	1 tbsp.	15 mL
Boneless, skinless chicken breast half, cut into 1/8 inch (3 mm) slices	5 – 6 oz.	140 – 170 g
Medium carrot, cut julienne	1	1
Cayenne pepper	1/8 tsp.	0.5 mL
Large red pepper, cut into 8 rings	1	1
Fresh bean sprouts	1 cup	250 mL
Green onions, thinly sliced	3	3
Sesame seeds, toasted (see Note)	1 tsp.	5 mL

Food Processor Method: Measure first 4 ingredients into food processor fitted with dough blade. With motor running, pour hot water and first amount of cooking oil through food chute. Process for 1 minute. If dough seems sticky, turn out onto lightly floured surface. Knead for about 5 minutes, adding more flour as needed, until smooth and elastic. Cover with tea towel. Let dough rest for 15 minutes.

Hand Method: Combine first 4 ingredients in medium bowl. Add hot water and first amount of cooking oil. Mix well until dough pulls away from side of bowl. Turn out onto lightly floured surface. Knead for 5 to 8 minutes until smooth and elastic. Cover with tea towel. Let dough rest for 15 minutes.

To Complete: Roll out and press dough into greased 12 inch (30 cm) pizza pan, forming rim around edge. Spread with peanut sauce. Sprinkle with cheese.

(continued on next page)

Heat second amount of cooking oil in frying pan on medium. Add chicken, carrot and cayenne pepper. Cook for about 5 minutes, stirring often, until chicken is no longer pink. Arrange over cheese.

Place red pepper around outside edge. Bake on bottom rack in 425°F (220°C) oven for about 15 minutes until cheese is melted and crust is golden. Remove from oven.

Sprinkle with bean sprouts, green onion and sesame seeds. Cuts into 8 wedges.

1 wedge: 204 Calories; 8.2 g Total Fat (3.7 g Mono, 2 g Poly, 2 g Sat); 17 mg Cholesterol; 22 g Carbohydrate; 2 g Fibre; 11 g Protein; 359 mg Sodium

Pictured below.

The little sesame seeds cling well while chicken is cooking. Looks attractive.

notes

To toast sesame seeds, place in single layer in ungreased shallow pan. Bake in 350°F (175°C) oven for 5 to 10 minutes, stirring or shaking often, until desired doneness.

If desired, remove skin from chicken before dipping, to reduce fat.

Sesame Chicken

Fine soda cracker crumbs	1 cup	250 mL
Sesame seeds, toasted (see Note)	1/2 cup	125 mL
Paprika	1 tsp.	5 mL
Onion salt	1/2 tsp.	2 mL
Salt	3/4 tsp.	4 mL
Pepper	1/4 tsp.	1 mL
Bone-in chicken parts (see Note)	3 lbs.	1.4 kg
Milk	1/2 cup	125 mL

Combine first 6 ingredients in shallow dish.

Dip chicken in milk, then coat with crumb mixture. Arrange chicken, skin-side up, in single layer on greased baking sheet with sides. Bake in 375°F (190°C) oven for 30 minutes. Turn chicken. Bake for about 30 minutes until tender. Serves 4 to 6.

1 serving: 718 Calories; 47.3 g Total Fat (19.5 g Mono, 12.1 g Poly, 12 g Sat); 175 mg Cholesterol; 22 g Carbohydrate; 4 g Fibre; 50 g Protein; 1056 mg Sodium

Pictured below and on back cover.

Cantonese Chicken

Bone-in chicken parts (see Note)	3 lbs.	1.4 kg
Ketchup	1/2 cup	125 mL
Soy sauce	3 tbsp.	50 mL
Liquid honey	3 tbsp.	50 mL
Lemon juice	2 tbsp.	30 mL
Water	2 tbsp.	30 mL

Arrange chicken, skin-side down, in single layer in ungreased small roaster or 9 x 13 inch (22 x 33 cm) pan.

Combine remaining 5 ingredients in small bowl. Spoon over chicken. Cover. Marinate in refrigerator for at least 1 hour, turning once. Bake, covered, in 375°F (190°C) oven for 30 minutes. Baste chicken. Turn over. Bake, uncovered, for about 30 minutes until tender. Serves 4 to 6.

1 serving: 590 Calories; 35 g Total Fat (14.5 g Mono, 7.5 g Poly, 10 g Sat); 174 mg Cholesterol; 24 g Carbohydrate; trace Fibre; 45 g Protein; 1322 mg Sodium

Pictured below.

Cook this right in the marinade. A fantastic glaze.

note

If desired, remove skin from chicken before placing in roaster, to reduce fat.

serving suggestion

Serve over stir-fried vegetables.

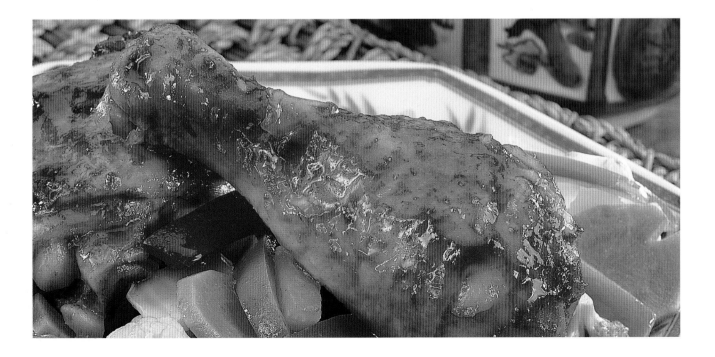

On your busiest workday, this dish can be on the table in under 30 minutes from start to finish.

serving suggestion

Make this a complete meal with steamed snow peas tossed with toasted sesame seeds and jasmine rice mixed with thinly sliced green onion.

Aniseed Chicken

Cooking oil	1 tbsp.	15 mL
Boneless, skinless chicken thighs (about 1 3/4 lbs., 790 g)	8	8
Garlic cloves, crushed (or 1/2 tsp., 2 mL, powder)	2	2
Finely grated gingerroot	1 tbsp.	15 mL
Prepared chicken broth	1/4 cup	60 mL
Liquid honey	1/4 cup	60 mL
Low-sodium soy sauce	3 tbsp.	50 mL
Chinese cooking wine (or dry sherry)	1 tbsp.	15 mL
Star anise	1	1
Coarse ground pepper	1/2 tsp.	2 mL
Water	1 tbsp.	15 mL
Cornstarch	1 1/2 tsp.	7 mL

Heat cooking oil in wok or large frying pan on medium-high. Cook chicken, in 2 batches, for about 3 minutes per side until lightly browned. Remove from wok.

Add garlic and ginger to same wok. Heat and stir for about 1 minute until fragrant.

Add next 6 ingredients. Bring to a boil on high. Reduce heat to medium-high. Add chicken. Cover. Cook for 10 to 15 minutes until chicken is no longer pink inside. Remove and discard star anise.

Stir water into cornstarch in small bowl until smooth. Stir into chicken mixture. Heat and stir for 1 to 2 minutes until sauce is boiling and thickened. Serves 4.

1 serving: 377 Calories; 14.2 g Total Fat (5.4 g Mono, 3.7 g Poly, 3 g Sat); 164 mg Cholesterol; 22 g Carbohydrate; trace Fibre; 39 g Protein; 345 mg Sodium

Pictured on page 109.

Faintly reminiscent of sweet and sour chicken.

note

If desired, remove skin from chicken before placing in pan, to reduce fat.

Chicken Diable

Hard margarine (or butter)	1/4 cup	60 mL
Liquid honey	1/4 cup	60 mL
Corn syrup (or honey)	1/4 cup	60 mL
Prepared mustard	1/4 cup	60 mL
Curry powder	1 tsp.	5 mL
Salt	1 tsp.	5 mL
Bone-in chicken parts (see Note)	3 lbs.	1.4 kg

Combine first 6 ingredients in small saucepan. Heat and stir on medium until margarine is melted.

Arrange chicken, skin-side up, in single layer in ungreased 9 x 13 inch (22 x 33 cm) pan. Pour honey mixture over top, making sure each piece is coated. Bake, uncovered, in 375°F (190°C) oven for about 1 hour until tender. Serves 4 to 6.

1 serving: 762 Calories; 47.9 g Total Fat (18.5 g Mono, 8.1 g Poly, 17.6 g Sat); 207 mg Cholesterol; 40 g Carbohydrate; trace Fibre; 44 g Protein; 1108 mg Sodium

Pictured on page 112.

Just two ingredients and as many minutes finds this in the oven. A long-time favourite.

note

If desired, remove skin from chicken before placing in roaster, to reduce fat.

Speedy Chicken

Bone-in chicken parts (see Note)	3 lbs.	1.4 kg
Envelope of dry onion soup mix	1 1/2 oz.	42 g

Arrange chicken, skin-side up, in single layer on greased foil in small roaster. Sprinkle evenly with soup mix. Fold foil over top. Cover roaster. Bake in 350°F (175°C) oven for 1 1/2 to 2 hours until tender. Serves 4 to 6.

1 serving: 529 Calories; 35.5 g Total Fat (14.9 g Mono, 7.6 g Poly, 10.1 g Sat); 174 mg Cholesterol; 6 g Carbohydrate; trace Fibre; 44 g Protein; 1114 mg Sodium

Pictured on page 112.

Chicken In Cream

Hard margarine (butter browns too fast)	1/4 cup	60 mL
Bone-in chicken parts (see Note)	3 lbs.	1.4 kg
Medium onion, sliced	1	1
Whipping cream	1 1/2 cups	375 mL

Melt margarine in large frying pan on medium. Add chicken. Cook for about 10 minutes, turning several times, until browned. Remove from pan.

Add onion to same frying pan. Cook for 5 to 10 minutes, stirring often, until softened. Add more margarine, if needed. Add chicken.

Pour whipping cream over top. Reduce heat. Cover. Simmer gently on medium-low for 20 to 30 minutes until chicken is tender. Serves 4 to 6.

1 serving: 763 Calories; 65.2 g Total Fat (24.7 g Mono, 7.7 g Poly, 28.5 g Sat); 254 mg Cholesterol; 5 g Carbohydrate; trace Fibre; 38 g Protein; 238 mg Sodium

Pictured on page 113.

A simple and delicious Ukrainian recipe.

note

If desired, remove skin from chicken before cooking, to reduce fat.

Golden Glazed Chicken

Liquid honey	1/4 cup	60 mL
Prepared mustard	1/4 cup	60 mL
Dried tarragon leaves	1 tsp.	5 mL
Bone-in chicken parts (see Note)	2 1/2 lbs.	1.1 kg

Combine honey, mustard and tarragon in small bowl.

Arrange chicken, skin-side up, in single layer in small roaster. Spoon sauce over top, making sure each piece is coated. Bake, uncovered, in 350°F (175°C) oven for about 1 hour until tender. Remove chicken to warm platter. Spoon sauce over top. Serves 4.

1 serving: 578 Calories; 30.3 g Total Fat (5.8 g Mono, 3.1 g Poly, 3.7 g Sat); 110 mg Cholesterol; 23 g Carbohydrate; trace Fibre; 52 g Protein; 269 mg Sodium

Pictured on page 113.

So tasty and attractive.

note

If desired, remove skin from chicken before placing in roaster, to reduce fat.

Pictured on Next Page:
Top Left: Speedy Chicken, page 110
Top Right: Golden Glazed Chicken, this page
Bottom Right: Chicken In Cream, this page
Bottom Left: Chicken Diable, page 110

A real winner. So simple to assemble, it is hard to believe it ends up as a gourmet dish.

Bev's Chicken Casserole

Bone-in chicken parts, skin removed	3 lbs.	1.4 kg
Garlic powder	3/4 tsp.	4 mL
Salt	1 tsp.	5 mL
Pepper	1/4 tsp.	1 mL
Can of condensed tomato soup	10 oz.	284 mL
Can of condensed cream of mushroom soup	10 oz.	284 mL
Green onions (about 1 bunch), thinly sliced	7 – 9	7 – 9
Small onion, chopped	1	1
Medium tomato, chopped	1	1

Arrange chicken in single layer in ungreased 3 quart (3 L) casserole or small roaster. Sprinkle with garlic, salt and pepper.

Combine remaining 5 ingredients in medium bowl. Spoon over chicken. Cover. Bake in 350°F (175°C) oven for about 2 hours until tender. Serves 4 to 6.

1 serving: 308 Calories; 11.2 g Total Fat (2.6 g Mono, 4.3 g Poly, 2.9 g Sat); 96 mg Cholesterol; 19 g Carbohydrate; 2 g Fibre; 32 g Protein; 1837 mg Sodium

Pictured on page 115.

A coating flavoured with thyme. Crispy like its name.

Crispy Chicken

All-purpose flour	3/4 cup	175 mL
Paprika	1 tsp.	5 mL
Ground thyme	1 tsp.	5 mL
Salt	1 tsp.	5 mL
Pepper	1/4 tsp.	1 mL
Large egg	1	1
Milk	2 tbsp.	30 mL
Lemon juice	2 tsp.	10 mL
Bone-in chicken parts	3 lbs.	1.4 kg
Hard margarine (or butter), melted	1/4 cup	60 mL

(continued on next page)

Measure first 5 ingredients into shallow dish. Mix.

Beat egg in separate shallow dish. Add milk and lemon juice. Stir.

Dip chicken into flour mixture, then into egg mixture. Dip back into flour mixture until coated. Arrange chicken, skin-side up, in single layer on greased baking sheet. Let stand for 30 minutes.

Drizzle with margarine. Bake in 350°F (175°C) oven for 1 to 1 1/4 hours until tender. Serves 4 to 6.

1 serving: 722 Calories; 48.8 g Total Fat (18.5 g Mono, 8.3 g Poly, 18.1 g Sat); 261 mg Cholesterol; 20 g Carbohydrate; trace Fibre; 48 g Protein; 901 mg Sodium

Pictured below.

Top Left: Crispy Chicken, page 114
Bottom Right: Bev's Chicken Casserole, page 114

Chicken with a dark sauce that is absolutely fantastic. You will want to make extra for sure.

Holiday Chicken

Bone-in chicken parts, skin removed	4 lbs.	1.8 kg
Can of whole cranberry sauce	14 oz.	398 mL
Granulated sugar	1/3 cup	75 mL
White vinegar	1/4 cup	60 mL
Envelope dry onion soup mix	1 1/2 oz.	42 g
Chili sauce	3 tbsp.	50 mL
Cooking oil	2 tbsp.	30 mL

Fresh (or frozen) cranberries, for garnish

Arrange chicken in single layer in ungreased medium roaster.

Combine next 6 ingredients in small bowl. Spoon over chicken, making sure each piece is coated. Cover. Bake in 350°F (175°C) oven for about 1 1/2 hours until tender. Remove chicken to warm platter. Spoon sauce over top.

Garnish with cranberries. Serves 6 to 8.

1 serving: 407 Calories; 9.6 g Total Fat (4.3 g Mono, 2.5 g Poly, 1.6 g Sat); 102 mg Cholesterol; 48 g Carbohydrate; 2 g Fibre; 32 g Protein; 877 mg Sodium

Pictured on page 117.

A good sauce makes all the difference.

Duck With Plum Sauce

Whole young duck, quartered	5 lbs.	2.3 kg
PLUM SAUCE		
Jars of strained plums baby food (4 1/2 oz., 128 mL, each)	2	2
Apple cider vinegar	2 1/2 tbsp.	37 mL
Brown sugar, packed	2 tbsp.	30 mL
Ground cloves	1/8 tsp.	0.5 mL

Arrange duck, skin-side up, in single layer in medium roaster. Cover. Bake in 350°F (175°C) oven for 1 to 1 1/2 hours until tender. Drain.

Plum Sauce: Combine all 4 ingredients in small bowl. Makes 1 cup (250 mL) sauce. Brush sauce over duck. Bake, uncovered, for 10 minutes. Brush with sauce. Bake for about 5 minutes until glazed. Remove duck to warm platter. Spoon remaining sauce over top. Serves 4.

1 serving: 809 Calories; 61.4 g Total Fat (27.9 g Mono, 7.9 g Poly, 20.9 g Sat); 182 mg Cholesterol; 21 g Carbohydrate; trace Fibre; 42 g Protein; 138 mg Sodium

Pictured on page 117.

Top: Holiday Chicken, above
Bottom: Duck With Plum Sauce, above

A meal with flair when you serve an individual bird to each guest.

Cornish Hens

WILD RICE STUFFING

Box of long grain and wild rice mix	6 1/4 oz.	180 g
Hard margarine (or butter)	2 tbsp.	30 mL
Chopped celery	1/2 cup	125 mL
Chopped onion	1/2 cup	125 mL
Can of mushroom stems and pieces, drained	10 oz.	284 mL
Poultry seasoning	1/2 tsp.	2 mL
Salt	1/2 tsp.	2 mL
Cornish hens (about 1 lb., 454 g, each)	4	4
Red currant jelly (or orange marmalade)	1/4 cup	60 mL

Wild Rice Stuffing: Cook rice according to package directions. Put into medium bowl.

Melt margarine in frying pan on medium. Add celery and onion. Cook for 5 to 10 minutes, stirring often, until softened.

Add mushrooms, poultry seasoning and salt. Stir. Add to cooked rice. Mix well. Makes about 3 1/2 cups (875 mL) stuffing.

Loosely fill body cavity of each hen with stuffing. Secure with wooden picks or small metal skewers. Tie wings close to body. Tie legs to tail. Put into large roaster. Cover. Bake in 350°F (175°C) oven for 45 minutes.

Brush hens with jelly. Bake, uncovered, for 30 to 45 minutes until tender. Makes 4 stuffed hens.

1 stuffed hen: 963 Calories; 53.6 g Total Fat (22.4 g Mono, 9.7 g Poly, 17.1 g Sat); 351 mg Cholesterol; 54 g Carbohydrate; 3 g Fibre; 64 g Protein; 768 mg Sodium

Pictured on page 119.

What a wonderful stuffing surprise inside! There is quite a difference in flavour (and cost) between the prosciutto and ham. Choose your preference.

Stuffed Turkey Scaloppine

Lean prosciutto (or cooked ham), chopped	4 oz.	113 g
Grated part-skim mozzarella cheese	1/2 cup	125 mL
Chopped fresh parsley (or 3/4 tsp., 4 mL, flakes)	1 tbsp.	15 mL
Chopped fresh basil (or 3/4 tsp., 4 mL, dried)	1 tbsp.	15 mL
Garlic clove, minced (or 1/4 tsp., 1 mL, powder)	1	1
Thin turkey scaloppine	1 lb.	454 g
Can of Italian plum tomatoes (with juice), chopped	28 oz.	796 mL
Granulated sugar	1 tsp.	5 mL
Dried sweet basil	1 tsp.	5 mL
Dried oregano	1/2 tsp.	2 mL
Pepper	1/4 tsp.	1 mL
Spaghetti	8 oz.	225 g
Boiling water	8 cups	2 L
Salt (optional)	1 tsp.	5 mL
Water	1 tbsp.	15 mL
Cornstarch	1 tbsp.	15 mL

Combine first 5 ingredients in small bowl.

Pound turkey with flat side of mallet to 1/4 inch (6 mm) thickness. Cut into 8 serving-size pieces. Place about 3 tbsp. (50 mL) prosciutto mixture on narrow end of each turkey piece. Roll up, tucking in sides. Secure with wooden picks or tie with butcher's string. Heat lightly greased large non-stick frying pan on medium. Brown rolls on all sides until golden.

Add next 5 ingredients. Stir. Reduce heat. Cover. Simmer for 30 minutes. Remove rolls to plate. Cover to keep warm.

Cook spaghetti in boiling water and salt in large uncovered pot or Dutch oven for 7 to 9 minutes until tender but firm. Drain. Put into large serving bowl.

Stir water into cornstarch in small cup until smooth. Add to tomato mixture. Heat and stir on medium until boiling and slightly thickened. Makes 3 cups (750 mL) sauce. Pour over spaghetti. Toss gently. Serve with turkey rolls. Serves 4.

1 serving: 150 Calories; 5.3 g Total Fat (2.1 g Mono, 0.8 g Poly, 2 g Sat); 27 mg Cholesterol; 14 g Carbohydrate; 1 g Fibre; 12 g Protein; 234 mg Sodium

Pictured on page 121.

The cranberry stuffing imparts a tart, but subtle, sweetness. A very impressive presentation. This may look complicated and fussy, but is really very easy.

Stuffed Turkey Breast

SPICED CRANBERRY STUFFING

Hard margarine (or butter)	1/4 cup	60 mL
Chopped onion	1/2 cup	125 mL
Chopped celery	1/2 cup	125 mL
Garlic cloves, minced (or 1/2 tsp., 2 mL, powder), optional	2	2
Chopped cranberries	2/3 cup	150 mL
Grated peeled tart cooking apple (such as Granny Smith)	1/2 cup	125 mL
Fine dry bread crumbs	1/2 cup	125 mL
Brown sugar, packed	1 tbsp.	15 mL
Ground cinnamon	1/4 tsp.	1 mL
Ground nutmeg	1/8 tsp.	0.5 mL
Ground allspice	1/8 tsp.	0.5 mL
Cayenne pepper	1/8 tsp.	0.5 mL
Salt	1/2 tsp.	2 mL
Pepper	1/8 tsp.	0.5 mL
Apple juice (or water),	1 tbsp.	15 mL
Whole turkey breast, bone-in (see Note)	6 lbs.	2.7 kg
Hard margarine (or butter), melted	2 tbsp.	30 mL
Seasoned salt	1/2 tsp.	2 mL
Pepper, sprinkle		

Spiced Cranberry Stuffing: Melt margarine in large frying pan on medium. Add onion, celery and garlic. Cook for 5 to 10 minutes, stirring often, until onion is softened. Remove form heat.

Add next 10 ingredients. Mix well.

Add enough apple juice until stuffing is moist and holds together when squeezed.

(continued on next page)

Cut turkey crosswise into 1 inch (2.5 cm) thick slices right to bone on both sides. You should be able to cut about 6 slices on each side. Use very sharp knife to keep skin intact. Divide stuffing among "pockets" cut into turkey. Tie butcher's string horizontally around turkey once or twice to hold slices with stuffing together. Place turkey, cut side up, in medium roasting pan.

Drizzle second amount of margarine over turkey. Sprinkle with seasoned salt and second amount of pepper. Cover. Cook in 325°F (160°C) oven for 1 3/4 to 2 hours, basting turkey several times with juices from bottom of roasting pan, until meat thermometer reads 180°F (82°C). Increase heat to 400°F (205°C). Remove cover. Cook for about 15 minutes until skin is browned. Serves 10 to 12.

1 serving: 404 Calories; 13.9 g Total Fat (7.2 g Mono, 2.3 g Poly, 3.3 g Sat); 168 mg Cholesterol; 9 g Carbohydrate; 1 g Fibre; 58 g Protein; 433 mg Sodium

Pictured below.

Throughout this book measurements are given in Conventional and Metric measure. To compensate for differences between the two measurements due to rounding, a full metric measure is not always used. The cup used is the standard 8 fluid ounce. Temperature is given in degrees Fahrenheit and Celsius. Baking pan measurements are in inches and centimetres as well as quarts and litres. An exact metric conversion is given on this page as well as the working equivalent (Metric Standard Measure).

Pans

Conventional – Inches	Metric – Centimetres
8 × 8 inch	20 × 20 cm
9 × 9 inch	22 × 22 cm
9 × 13 inch	22 × 33 cm
10 × 15 inch	25 × 38 cm
11 × 17 inch	28 × 43 cm
8 × 2 inch round	20 × 5 cm
9 × 2 inch round	22 × 5 cm
10 × 4 1/2 inch tube	25 × 11 cm
8 × 4 × 3 inch loaf	20 × 10 × 7.5 cm
9 × 5 × 3 inch loaf	22 × 12.5 × 7.5 cm

Oven Temperatures

Fahrenheit (°F)	Celsius (°C)	Fahrenheit (°F)	Celsius (°C)
175°	80°	350°	175°
200°	95°	375°	190°
225°	110°	400°	205°
250°	120°	425°	220°
275°	140°	450°	230°
300°	150°	475°	240°
325°	160°	500°	260°

Spoons

Conventional Measure	Metric Exact Conversion Millilitre (mL)	Metric Standard Measure Millilitre (mL)
1/8 teaspoon (tsp.)	0.6 mL	0.5 mL
1/4 teaspoon (tsp.)	1.2 mL	1 mL
1/2 teaspoon (tsp.)	2.4 mL	2 mL
1 teaspoon (tsp.)	4.7 mL	5 mL
2 teaspoons (tsp.)	9.4 mL	10 mL
1 tablespoon (tbsp.)	14.2 mL	15 mL

Dry Measurements

Conventional Measure Ounces (oz.)	Metric Exact Conversion Grams (g)	Metric Standard Measure Grams (g)
1 oz.	28.3 g	28 g
2 oz.	56.7 g	57 g
3 oz.	85.0 g	85 g
4 oz.	113.4 g	125 g
5 oz.	141.7 g	140 g
6 oz.	170.1 g	170 g
7 oz.	198.4 g	200 g
8 oz.	226.8 g	250 g
16 oz.	453.6 g	500 g
32 oz.	907.2 g	1000 g (1 kg)

Cups

1/4 cup (4 tbsp.)	56.8 mL	60 mL
1/3 cup (5 1/3 tbsp.)	75.6 mL	75 mL
1/2 cup (8 tbsp.)	113.7 mL	125 mL
2/3 cup (10 2/3 tbsp.)	151.2 mL	150 mL
3/4 cup (12 tbsp.)	170.5 mL	175 mL
1 cup (16 tbsp.)	227.3 mL	250 mL
4 1/2 cups	1022.9 mL	1000 mL (1 L)

Casseroles

Canada & Britain		United States	
Standard Size Casserole	Exact Metric Measure	Standard Size Casserole	Exact Metric Measure
1 qt. (5 cups)	1.13 L	1 qt. (4 cups)	900 mL
1 1/2 qts. (7 1/2 cups)	1.69 L	1 1/2 qts. (6 cups)	1.35 L
2 qts. (10 cups)	2.25 L	2 qts. (8 cups)	1.8 L
2 1/2 qts. (12 1/2 cups)	2.81 L	2 1/2 qts. (10 cups)	2.25 L
3 qts. (15 cups)	3.38 L	3 qts. (12 cups)	2.7 L
4 qts. (20 cups)	4.5 L	4 qts. (16 cups)	3.6 L
5 qts. (25 cups)	5.63 L	5 qts. (20 cups)	4.5 L

tip index